Your Personal Invitation to the Ultimate Celebrity Roast

George Burns on Carol Channing: "Carol never just enters a room. Even when she comes out of the bathroom her husband applauds."

Mr. Blackwell on Dustin Hoffman: "Better as a woman. If I were him, I'd never get out of drag."

Carol Burnett on Burt Reynolds: "I'm in bed with Burt Reynolds most of the time in the play. Oh, I know it's dirty work, but somebody has to do it."

Carson lashes out at Rona, Andy Rooney lampoons Yves Saint Laurent, and Joan Rivers ridicules Richard Simmons. Here is a star-studded collection of 1,500 insults, put-downs, zingers, and back-stabs that ricochet from celebrity to celebrity from the annals of Hollywood and history.

Find your favorite celebrities and what's being said about them in:

THE BEDSIDE BOOK OF

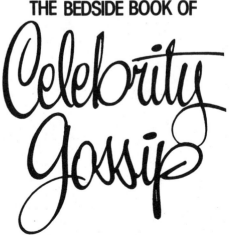

Celebrity Gossip

THE BEDSIDE BOOK OF

Celebrity Gossip

1,500 Outrageous Barbs from One Celebrity to Another

CELEBRITY RESEARCH GROUP

Prince Paperbacks
Crown Publishers, Inc.
New York

To R.S.
We still have only good to say of you.

Copyright © 1984 by the Celebrity Research Group, Inc.

A Prince Paperback Book
Published by Crown Publishers, Inc., One Park Avenue, New York, New York 10016 and simultaneously in Canada by General Publishing Company Limited

PRINCE PAPERBACKS and colophon are trademarks of Crown Publishers, Inc.

Manufactured in the United States of America

Library of Congress Cataloging in Publication Data
Main entry under title:
The Bedside book of celebrity gossip.
1. Quotations, English.   2. Biography—Anecdotes, facetiae, satire, etc.   3. Wit and humor.   I. Title:
Celebrity gossip.
PN6084.H8B42   1984   082   83-18814
ISBN 0-517-55172-1
10 9 8 7 6 5 4 3 2 1
FIRST EDITION

Gossip is dangerous in direct proportion to the gullibility of the audience.

Jonathan Miller

Vitriol in Fun

What's gossip? Does it always have to be negative? Why do people always want to hear the worst about others, when the best about them is infinitely more encouraging?

1. *What's gossip?* Gossip, from the Anglo-Saxon *godsibb*, originally meant God *(god)* relation *(sibb)*, for instance, a godparent, one who was particularly charged to look out for the interests of the godchild. From that, it expanded to mean any kind of friend or crony. And from that—Wouldn't you just know it?—it came to mean the sort of things said behind other people's backs. Why? Ask your godparents. If they don't know, your friends are bound to.

2. *Does it have to be negative?* See above. Then ask yourself how you'd feel if this turned out to be a collection of celebrity compliments.

3. *Why the worst when the best is more encouraging?* But is it? Isn't there something fundamentally satisfying in knowing that no one is immune from bad-mouthing? The most extreme public name-calling today pales by comparison to the vilifications heaped on Mahatma Gandhi and George Washington in their day. Before the advent of mass media, elections were fought and won on the basis of malicious slurs delivered as fact to voters who had no way of knowing the "facts" were patently untrue. In our own time, we've seen more accuracy, more restraint, yet some prominent hands are far from clean. There was the candidate who pretty effectively cast aspersions on his

opponent by declaring the man's wife a "practicing thespian." Indeed she was—she was a paid, professional *actress!* And then there was the time Richard Nixon exhorted a crowd to avoid political inertia. "We can't stand pat," he told them. It wasn't long before the newspaper headline appeared—"Nixon: Can't Stand Pat."

Meaning what?

Meaning not all gossip is fair. Or accurate.

Frequently, it reflects on its speaker more than on its intended target. (This is the you're-rubber-and-I'm-glue/Whatever-you-say-bounces-off-me-and-sticks-to-you variety.)

Neither is gossip carved in stone. Life is long. People's opinions change about other people. When Clark Gable was first making screen tests in Hollywood, the director who didn't turn him down with a snappy crack about his ears was considered a dullard. When Gable went on to prove his stuff as the box-office king of Hollywood, they changed their tunes. George Raft had no use for movie newcomer Ingrid Bergman, nor the movie he was offered the lead in, and unceremoniously dismissed them both. The part went to Humphrey Bogart. The movie was *Casablanca.* Soon after, Raft was gentleman enough to eat his words.

As Billie Jean King has said, "I change my mind so often that whatever the situation is, it's usually totally different by the time a particular item sees print."

If you can change your mind about liking someone—surely a universal experience—then you can just as easily change your mind about disliking someone. That's simply the way life is.

Sometimes personal remarks are intended as no more than observations. When David Niven described William Randolph Hearst as someone shaped like an avocado, it was not to imply that Hearst was green or lumpy—nor that it is more desirable to be shaped like an apple. It was doubtless an attempt to be accurate.

In this book you'll find entries ranging from the gentle nastiness emerging from friendly funning to those unrestrained vilifications that could cut glass. For instance, our Founding Fathers on the subject of other of our Founding Fathers. In between, there are the unintentionally chilling assessments like

Hedda Hopper's "tribute" to Joan Crawford's warm heart: "Whenever she came to the realization that the men she loved simply didn't love back, she compensated for these emotional setbacks by adopting four children"; along with intentionally devastating denouncements from critics of dubious qualification, as for example, "I have tried lately to read Shakespeare, and found it so intolerably dull that it nauseated me," said by Charles Darwin.

In this book, you will find quotations from famous people of past and present. If you like what they say, by all means don't restrict yourself to what's between these covers. Researching *The Bedside Book of Celebrity Gossip* has made us walking advertisements for the works of hundreds of celebrities. So much the better. For them, and—if you pursue it—for you.

What this book does not contain nor pretend to contain is well-rounded biographical information. Nor—because it is the printed rather than the spoken word—can it give the inflections with which certain sentiments were delivered. This is to say that, while nothing has been taken deliberately out of context, reading remarks is not the same as being there.

Finally, *The Bedside Book of Celebrity Gossip* is a collection of facts only in the sense that, in fact, these things were said (or written) by these people at some point in time.

If these people also happen to be thespians, that's their business.

Our business is to offer this collection of quotations, some all in fun, some not so funny, encouraged (there's that word again) by the notion that when even being great and famous doesn't preclude being called pond scum, there's hope for us all.

DEAN ACHESON
"To French ears Dean Acheson sounds like one of those physicians immortalised by Molière, who do not wish the patient to get better."
—PETER USTINOV

JOEY AND CINDY ADAMS
"John and Quincy Adams" —MILTON BERLE

JOHN ADAMS
"One of those Protestants who do not believe in anything."
—JOHN ADAMS

"He is distrustful, obstinate, excessively vain, and takes no counsel from anyone." —THOMAS JEFFERSON

"It has been the political career of this man to begin with hypocrisy, proceed with arrogance, and finish with contempt."
—THOMAS PAINE

CHARLES ADDAMS
"I'd always joked with him that he would spawn with anything that twitched." —JOAN FONTAINE

SPIRO AGNEW
"Has become what we all once took some joy in deriding: a nattering nabob of negativism." —WILLIAM SAFIRE

"The deal for Agnew's light sentence was made in a motel room. That makes motel rooms have one more evil meaning." —MORT SAHL

LOUISA MAY ALCOTT
"Though I was a devout Alcott groupie, I had to admit that she was zilch on sex. Very big at drawing discreet curtains, very big at leaving discreet intervals, she was forever dropping a row of asterisks exactly where you didn't want them . . ." —PEG BRACKEN

NELSON ALGREN
"His appearance is that of a horse player, who, this moment, got the news; he had bet her across the board and she came in a strong fourth." —STUDS TERKEL

1

MUHAMMAD ALI

"I have said I am the greatest. Ain't nobody ever heard me say I was the smartest."   —MUHAMMAD ALI

"If you doubt that the child shows the man, consider this: eighteen-month-old Cassius Clay [now Muhammad Ali] was being cuddled on Mummy's lap one day when a tiny fist shot straight up and knocked out one of Mummy's teeth."   —HARRIET VAN HORNE

FRED ALLEN

"My eyes look as though they are peeping over two dirty Ping-Pong balls."   —FRED ALLEN

STEVE ALLEN

"The jazz critics loved me as long as they thought I was black and dead."   —STEVE ALLEN

"When I can't sleep, I read a book by Steve Allen."
                    —OSCAR LEVANT

"I am fond of Steve Allen, but not as much as he is."
                    —JACK PAAR

WOODY ALLEN

"Woody Allen bought a poster of the underground classic *Bloodsucking Freaks* to dress up his office. Listen, some people prefer wallpaper."   —CINDY ADAMS

"A face that convinces you that God is a cartoonist."
                    —JACK KROLL

CHER BONO ALLMAN

"No mini's too short, no chiffon too sheer, no navel-baring T-shirt too tacky for Cher. She doesn't buy her clothes in the five and dime; our readers think she just looks that way."
                    —*US* ANNUAL READERS POLL, 1983

ROBERT ALTMAN

"Robert Altman films are usually terrible."   —JOAN CRAWFORD
                    (*See also:* Bernardo Bertolucci)

POUL ANDERSON

                    (*See entry:* Gordon Dickson)

2

URSULA ANDRESS
"The name has always seemed a spoonerism to me."
—JOHN SIMON

JULIE ANDREWS
"Working with her is like being hit over the head with a Valentine's card."
—CHRISTOPHER PLUMMER

YURI ANDROPOV
"Andropov is a modern computer filled with Russian software."
—HELMUT SCHMIDT

PRINCESS ANNE OF ENGLAND
"Such an active lass. So outdoorsy. She loves nature in spite of what it did to her."
—BETTE MIDLER

"The woman is a horse."
—JOAN RIVERS

ANN-MARGRET
"Almost antisexual cardboard-and-suet-meringue posturing . . ."
—JUDITH CRIST

JEAN ANOUILH
"For me, the two playwrights to be avoided at all costs are Brecht and Anouilh."
—ROBERT MORLEY

MARIE ANTOINETTE
(See entry: William Buckley)

SUSAN ANTON and DUDLEY MOORE
"She has hickies on her knees."
—JOAN RIVERS

YASSER ARAFAT
"Any leader can be a hero in victory; only Arafat could project himself as the hero of a catastrophe."
—JACK ANDERSON

"Arafat is so depressed he's been hanging around the house clean-shaven."
—JOHNNY CARSON

"That smirking monster with the manic grin on his face."
—JAMES J. KILPATRICK

ARISTOTLE
"Aristotle invented science, but destroyed philosophy."
—ALFRED NORTH WHITEHEAD

MATTHEW ARNOLD
"Poor Matt, he's gone to Heaven no doubt—but he won't like God."
—ROBERT LOUIS STEVENSON

ISAAC ASIMOV
"Why aren't you at home writing a book?"   —ALAN ALDA

"Isaac Asimov turned into a dirty old man at the age of fifteen."
—FREDERICK POHL

ED ASNER
"I don't know him well. But he seems an extremely angry and short-tempered man. He is enormously sensitive to criticism."
—CHARLTON HESTON

"My only problem with Ed Asner is that he speaks with the authority of Lou Grant and the brains of Ted Baxter."
—JOHN LEBOUTILLIER

MARGOT ASQUITH
"The affair between Margot Asquith and Margot Asquith will live as one of the prettiest love stories in all literature."
—DOROTHY PARKER

FRED ASTAIRE
"He is the nearest we are ever likely to get to a human Mickey [Mouse], near enough for many critics to have noted the resemblance."
—GRAHAM GREENE

"I am a little uncertain about the man, but I feel, in spite of his enormous ears and bad chin line, that his charm is so tremendous that it comes through . . . ."   —DAVID O. SELZNICK

JOHN JACOB ASTOR
"Mr. Astor, I am told, begun business in New York as a dealer in furs, and is now worth millions. Lord help the beavers and others! They must have got used to getting skinned by this time!"
—DAVY CROCKETT

LADY ASTOR
"I refuse to admit I'm more than fifty-two even if that does make my sons illegitimate."   —LADY ASTOR

ATTILA THE HUN
"I'm gonna be so tough as a mayor, I'm gonna make Attila the Hun look like a faggot."   —FRANK RIZZO

CLEMENT ATTLEE
"He is a sheep in sheep's clothing."   —WINSTON CHURCHILL

W. H. AUDEN
"A sort of gutless Kipling"   —GEORGE ORWELL

JEAN-PIERRE AUMONT
"Your accent is your main asset. I'd rather see you come back without a leg than without your accent."   —L. B. MAYER
(as Aumont left for war)

MARCUS AURELIUS
(*See entry:* Dorothy Parker)

JANE AUSTEN
"To me, Poe's prose is unreadable—like Jane Austen's. No, there is a difference. I would read his prose on a salary, but not Jane's."
—MARK TWAIN

GENE AUTRY
"Autry used to ride off into the sunset. Now he owns it."
—PAT BUTTRAM

"Please give my regards to your wife Dale."   —RICHARD NIXON

FRANKIE AVALON
"I was never sure if he had a sincere bone in his body. He was like a prostitute at heart. If you had the right price, you had him."
—RONA BARRETT

LAUREN BACALL
"If you want your coat held up, then don't act like a fella."
—HUMPHREY BOGART

"She simply is not aging as gracefully as Bette Davis."
—JACKIE COOPER

F. LEE BAILEY
"Who wants a lawyer who has glossies?"   —DAVID STEINBERG

BOBBY BAKER
"I never liked Bobby Baker, a negative reaction I could not ascribe to discriminating ethical standards, but it suggested much about my indifference to bragging fools."   —BARBARA HOWAR

CARROLL BAKER
"More bomb than bombshell"   —JUDITH CRIST

GEORGE BALANCHINE
"Why must everyone be 'great'? Isn't 'good' good enough? Everyone's overrated. Picasso's overrated. I'm overrated, even Jack Benny's overrated."   —GEORGE BALANCHINE

ARTHUR BALFOUR
"When Arthur Balfour launched his scheme for peopling Palestine with Jewish immigrants, I am credibly informed that he did not know there were Arabs in the country."   —DEAN WILLIAM R. INGE

HONORÉ DE BALZAC
"Can write the end of his book before he has finished the first paragraph, because he has turned all his creatures into clockwork cabbages and can rely on their staying put . . ."   —SAMUEL BECKETT

"I distrust a man who is capable of writing something approaching a hundred books."   —HENRY MILLER

"Balzac succeeds in giving the impression of greatness; in Tolstoi everything is great by nature—the droppings of an elephant beside those of a goat."   —MARCEL PROUST

TALLULAH BANKHEAD
"A parrot around Tallulah must feel as frustrated as a kleptomaniac in a piano store."   —FRED ALLEN

"As pure as the driven slush"   —TALLULAH BANKHEAD

"Miss Bankhead will never again act in a play of mine because I can only stand a certain amount of boredom."
                    —LILLIAN HELLMAN

"I've staged shows that called for the management of a herd of buffalo, and I've shot actors out of cannons for fifty feet into the arms of an adagio dancer, but both of them were easier than saying 'good morning' to Miss Bankhead."   —BILLY ROSE

"The first time I met her, I was in my dressing room, making up. Suddenly, I heard this sort of rustling, clumping noise behind me, and when I turned around, there was this totally naked woman. 'What's the matter, darling?' Tallulah said. 'Haven't you ever seen a blonde before?'"
—DONALD SUTHERLAND

"I suppose you could say Tallulah was a tramp, in the elegant sense."
—TENNESSEE WILLIAMS

"Talking so ceaselessly that you had to make a reservation five minutes ahead to get a word in."
—EARL WILSON

"Tallulah relishes being Tallulah Bankhead. She autographs pictures of herself, to herself, and presents them to herself."
—MAURICE ZOLOTOW

BARBIE DOLLS
"I had a Tressie doll, real cheap and gutterish. I liked her. I didn't like Barbie. She was too mainstream."
—SANDRA BERNHARD

BRIGITTE BARDOT
"I started out as a lousy actress and have remained one."
—BRIGITTE BARDOT

"The only thing this actress offers us in the way of change is the constant covering up and uncovering of her charming derrière."
—JUDITH CRIST

"She used to sulk in the morning when I had not been nice to her in her dreams."
—ROGER VADIM
(*See also:* Lew Burdette)

"MA" BARKER
"She had the most resourceful criminal brain of any man or woman I have observed, and she passed it all on to her sons."
—J. EDGAR HOOVER

CLIVE BARNES
"If I decide to stay around Broadway beyond the current season, it will be for the pleasure of throwing his fat limey posterior out in the street."
—DAVID MERRICK

RONA BARRETT
"She doesn't need a steak knife. Rona cuts her food with her tongue."
—JOHNNY CARSON

"Congress should give a medal to her husband for waking up every Sunday morning and looking at her." —FRANK SINATRA

(See also: Walter Cronkite)

CHUCK BARRIS
"The most boring man on TV . . . thumbs down"
—Results of *PEOPLE* Poll, 1980

JOHN BARRYMORE
"For a man who has been dead for fifteen years I am in remarkable health." —JOHN BARRYMORE

"Conspicuously unclean and smelled highly on many occasions."
—DAVID NIVEN

"He only called people he loved 'shits' . . ." —ANTHONY QUINN

JOHN BARRYMORE and ERROL FLYNN
"When I saw what they looked like in daylight my ulcer was cured."
—JACK WARNER

LIONEL BARRYMORE
"Uses words only to flog them. He makes them suffer."
—JOHN BARRYMORE

AUBREY BEARDSLEY
"His influence lowered taste and did not elevate it."
—*New York Times* Editorial, 1898

THE BEATLES
"I've said it before, and I say it again: when the British copy American they always copy the wrong things, from hamburgers to Beatles."
—JOHN O'HARA

"Although I plead guilty to having first inflicted the Beatles on America on my show, their appeal has always eluded me." —JACK PAAR

WARREN BEATTY
"Every time I go on a talk show, I am invariably asked about Warren Beatty's sex life. I have a stock answer: 'He should be in a jar at the Harvard Medical School.'" —JAMES BACON

"A post-graduate hypochondriac" —MIKE NICHOLS

"Interviewing Warren Beatty is like asking a hemophiliac for a pint of blood." —REX REED

SAMUEL BECKETT
"I took one look at his script and asked him if he ate Welsh rarebit before he went to bed at night."   —BUSTER KEATON

BEDE
"A bummer even by Dark Ages standards, a lousy Latinist and a monastery bore"   —WILFRID SHEED

MAX BEERBOHM
"The gods bestowed on Max the gift of perpetual old age."
—OSCAR WILDE

WALLACE BEERY
"He always made me feel uncomfortable."   —JACKIE COOPER

"A man who whispered filth in my ear while he ripped me almost in two"   —GLORIA SWANSON

MENACHEM BEGIN
"He has a tendency to treat the Palestinians with scorn, to look down on them almost as subhumans and to rationalize his abusive attitude toward them by categorizing all Palestinians as terrorists."
—JIMMY CARTER

"I think Menachem Begin is boring and an egomaniac."
—SALLY QUINN
(See also: Sam Donaldson)

BO BELINSKY
"Bo was an appealing rogue and it is good to see the wastrels of the world win one now and then."   —GENE AUTRY

JOHN BELUSHI
"A good man, but a bad boy"   —DAN AYKROYD

ROBERT BENCHLEY
"It took me fifteen years to discover that I had no talent for writing, but I couldn't give it up because by that time I was too famous."
—ROBERT BENCHLEY

"I blame Alexander Woollcott and Robert Benchley and Dorothy Parker for parenting the cutesy and cruel critics who carve up the theater we know now."   —MERCEDES McCAMBRIDGE

MME. BEN-GURION
"Madame Ben-Gurion was the most perfect example I've ever encountered of what is affectionately known as the Yiddishe mama."
—SIMONE SIGNORET

TONY BENN
"I've always said about Tony that he immatures with age."
—HAROLD WILSON

ARNOLD BENNETT
"Sort of a pig in clover" —D. H. LAWRENCE

JACK BENNY
"Jack Benny couldn't ad-lib a belch after a Hungarian dinner."
—FRED ALLEN

"Ladies and gentlemen, this is Jack Benny talking. There will be a slight pause while you say, 'Who cares?'" —JACK BENNY

"He never liked what he ordered, he only liked what you ordered."
—GEORGE BURNS
(See also: George Balanchine)

CANDICE BERGEN
"Joanna Shimkus is an Anglo-French Candice Bergen: a pretty girl who, by trying to act and failing, makes herself unpretty."
—STANLEY KAUFFMANN

"Since making her debut as Lakey the Lesbian in the film version of Mary McCarthy's *The Group*, Ms. Bergen has displayed the same emotional range and dramatic intensity as her father's dummy, Charlie McCarthy." —HARRY and MICHAEL MEDVED,
co-founders of the Golden Turkey Awards

INGMAR BERGMAN
"The only thing I have against Bergman, one of my gods, is that he's obtrusive. He's always telling you it's a Bergman film, a Bergman shot. Well I saw it, OK, Ingmar, we heard you. We all know you're there."
—MEL BROOKS

INGRID BERGMAN
"A reputation for being a terribly difficult interview"
—SALLY QUINN

"I don't want to star opposite an unknown Swedish broad."
—GEORGE RAFT

"I note Bergman is 69½ inches tall. Is it possible she is actually this high . . . ?"   —DAVID O. SELZNICK

MILTON BERLE

"Berle is a great comic. After all he's been on TV for years and I finally figured out the reason for his success—he's never improved."
—STEVE ALLEN

"If I accepted all the after-dinner speeches I'm asked to make, I'd spend half of my life eating chicken croquettes and sitting between Milton Berle and Jack Carter."   —GEORGE BURNS

"Berle is responsible for more television sets being sold than anyone else. I sold mine, my father sold his."   —JOE E. LEWIS

"I've seen you in dresses, so watch it."   —RICHARD PRYOR

"Lincoln would have loved him."   —CARL SANDBURG

HECTOR BERLIOZ

"At least I have the modesty to admit that lack of modesty is one of my failings."   —HECTOR BERLIOZ

SARAH BERNHARDT

"Any year after the invention of sound, film audiences could see her only as a figure of fun, a dumb creature jerking her sawdust heart around in a puppet world."   —ALISTAIR COOKE

CARL BERNSTEIN and BOB WOODWARD

"Reporters-turned-mindreaders"   —WILLIAM SAFIRE

YOGI BERRA

"Yogi's supposed to have said a lot of funny things, but I don't know how anyone hears all the things he says because he doesn't talk."
—SPARKY LYLE

BERNARDO BERTOLUCCI

"A clever, cheap exploiter of everything that comes to his hand, including the talent he began with (like Altman)"
—STANLEY KAUFFMANN

AMBROSE BIERCE

"Bierce would bury his best friend with a sigh of relief, and express satisfaction that he was done with him."   —JACK LONDON

11

BILLY THE KID
"Drank and laughed, rode and laughed, talked and laughed, fought and laughed, and killed and laughed" —PAT GARRETT

JIM BISHOP
"A very good second-rate writer" —BARBARA HOWAR

KAREN BLACK
(See entry: Norma Shearer)

LINDA BLAIR
"When I was your age, I was nineteen." —VICTOR BORGE

HUMPHREY BOGART
"He had two rules for playing with Method actors: (1) Let them improvise to their hearts' content and just wait for your cue; and (2) Don't ever play an eating scene with them, because they spit all over you." —NATHANIEL BENCHLEY

"Bogart's a helluva nice guy till 11:30 P.M. After that he thinks he's Bogart." —DAVE CHASEN

"An actor of consummate skill, with an ego to match" —WILLIAM HOLDEN

"I have to be up early to make sure the set is ready for prematurely balding and aging actors like you." —STANLEY KRAMER

"His first thought was, 'Let's have a drink.' His second was, 'Now, who can we louse up today? Let's get started.'" —EARL WILSON

HUMPHREY BOGART and MAYO METHOT
"Their neighbors were lulled to sleep by the sounds of breaking china and crashing glass." —DOROTHY PARKER

BJORN BORG
"I saw Bjorn in Las Vegas and asked him if he'd had any luck at the tables. He couldn't understand why I wanted to talk about furniture." —ARTHUR ASHE

"The only way he's going to hurt his arm is carrying his wallet." —VIC BRADEN

VICTOR BORGE
"Borge is a good pianist but he's no Horowitz. That should come as a relief to the parents of Horowitz." —VICTOR BORGE

"Except that he occasionally plays a few notes on the piano, he does less on stage than I do but to so much more effect."

—QUENTIN CRISP

MARTIN BORMANN
"Bormann was as addicted to alcohol as Goering was to drugs."

—ALBERT SPEER

CHARLES BOYER
"We've got a French actor here on a six-month option, but I'm letting him go because nobody can understand the guy's English."

—IRVING THALBERG

JOHANNES BRAHMS
"He excites and irritates our musical senses without wishing to satisfy them."

—PETER TCHAIKOVSKY

MARLON BRANDO
"I came out here with one suit and everybody thought I was a bum; when Brando came out with one sweat shirt, the town drooled over him."

—HUMPHREY BOGART

"Marlon Brando is so real, so humorous without any sense of humor."

—CHARLIE CHAPLIN

"I regard him as a supreme egotist."

—HEDDA HOPPER

"The choice of Marlon Brando as Marc Antony led some skeptics to quip that 'Friends, Romans, Countrymen' might become 'Kowalski Variations on a Speech by Shakespeare.'"

—JOHN HOUSEMAN

"Hurricane Marlon is sweeping the country, and I wish it were more than hot air."

—STANLEY KAUFFMANN

"The Indians never needed a lawyer until they got a benefactor like Marlon Brando."

—MORT SAHL

BERTOLT BRECHT
"Brecht has not only never had an original thought, he takes twice as long as the average playgoer to have any thought at all."

—ROBERT MORLEY

"I admit that, like Wagner, he is a great man: but I can't stand him at any cost."

—PETER USTINOV

(See also: Jean Anouilh)

LOUISE BROOKS
"Her favorite form of exercise was walking off a movie set, which she did with the insouciance of a little girl playing hopscotch."
—ANITA LOOS

MEL BROOKS
"The death of Hollywood is Mel Brooks and special effects. There is no humanity in films today. If Mel Brooks had come up in my generation, he wouldn't have qualified to be a busboy."
—JOSEPH MANKIEWICZ

"On a ha-ha level, Brooks is nothing short of a directorial disaster."
—ANDREW SARRIS

HEYWOOD BROUN
"Everything that touched him instantly—magically—lost its press."
—HARPO MARX

CHARLIE BROWN
"You are a foul ball in the line drive of life."   —LUCY VAN PELT

HELEN GURLEY BROWN
"If there had been Valley Girls in her day, the *Cosmo* editor would have been one to the max . . ."   —*PEOPLE*

JERRY BROWN
"Lord of the Flies"   —GORE VIDAL

ROBERT BROWNING
"Old Hippety-Hop o' the accents"   —EZRA POUND

"He has plenty of music in him, but he cannot get it out."
—ALFRED, LORD TENNYSON

LENNY BRUCE
"Lenny, despite what his cultists and the Dustin Hoffman movie said, was dirty and sick. He had no redeeming social values."
—JAMES BACON

WILLIAM JENNINGS BRYAN
"What animated him from end to end of his grotesque career was simply ambition—the ambition of a common man to get his hand upon the collar of his superiors, or, failing that, to get his thumb into their eyes."
—H. L. MENCKEN

"He is *absolutely* sincere. That is what makes him dangerous."
—WOODROW WILSON

ZBIGNIEW BRZEZINSKI
"A second-rate thinker in a field infested with poseurs and careerists, he has never let consistency get in the way of self-promotion or old theories impede new policy acrobatics."   —HODDING CARTER III

WILLIAM F. BUCKLEY, JR.
". . . a twisted and ignorant young man whose personal views of economics would have seemed reactionary to Mark Hanna"
—McGEORGE BUNDY

"The great thing about reading Buckley is that one comes to really understand why so gallant a nation as France lopped off so pretty a head as Marie Antoinette's. 'Let them eat cake' is an infuriating phrase in any language . . ."   —MARIO PUZO

"Probably the only person in the world who would work in a word like 'solipsistic'—while calling his dog"   —MARK RUSSELL

NIKOLAI BULGANIN
"That ridiculous toy soldier who tries to be marshal of the Red Army, but is only a fop in uniform"   —JOSEPH STALIN

LEW BURDETTE
"Burdette was told that he had trouble pitching on hot dry days and that he pitched like Brigitte Bardot walks—the only pitcher in baseball that could make coffee nervous."   —JOE GARAGIOLA

ANTHONY BURGESS
"A notorious literary careerist whose most obnoxious public stance is to put down those writers—like E. M. Forster and Saul Bellow—who are by light-years his superior."   —WILLIAM STYRON

GEORGE BURNS
"All the women my age are dead."   —GEORGE BURNS

"I've been speaking French all my life, and now after listening to you I find out I've been doing it all wrong."
—JACQUELINE KENNEDY ONASSIS

GEORGE BURNS, PHIL HARRIS, and DEAN MARTIN
"Me without ketchup is like Dean Martin splitting a milk shake with Phil Harris."   —GEORGE BURNS

GEORGE BURNS, LAWRENCE WELK, VINCENTE MINNELLI,
and BOB HOPE
"For excitement on Saturday night in North Hollywood, George
Burns, Lawrence Welk, Vincente Minnelli, and I sit around and watch
to see whose leg falls asleep faster—then we try to contact the living."
—BOB HOPE

AARON BURR
"The truth is, nobody is to be consoled for his loss, no respect is to be
entertained for the memory of one so profilgate in private and publick
life." —Obituary, *New York Evening Post*
(See also: Joseph McCarthy)

RICHARD BURTON
"Richard Burton seems to be announcing his availability for Vincent
Price roles." —GARY ARNOLD

"Richard Burton once drank a quart of brandy during his performance
of *Hamlet* on Broadway. The only visible effect was that he played the
last two acts as a homosexual." —JAMES BACON

"Richard Burton, once an actor, now performs mainly as a buffoon."
—JAY COCKS

"There is no longer any novelty in watching the sad disintegration of
Richard Burton's acting career." —ROGER EBERT

"Who could take that scruffy, arrogant buffoon seriously?"
—EDDIE FISHER

"Richard Burton is so discriminating that he won't go to see a play
with anybody in it but himself." —ELIZABETH TAYLOR

"One of the hardest chores for me as an actress is to have to simulate
real feeling in love senes when there is no chemistry between me and
the leading man." —LANA TURNER

RICHARD BURTON AND ELIZABETH TAYLOR
"Who wants to be a legendary drinker married to a wife who can drink
you under the table?" —JAMES BACON

GEORGE GORDON, LORD BYRON
"Except for his genius he was an ordinary nineteenth-century English
gentleman, with little culture and no ideas." —MATTHEW ARNOLD

"A wicked lord, who, from morbid and restless vanity, pretended to be ten times more wicked than he was."
—SAMUEL TAYLOR COLERIDGE

"The world is rid of Lord Byron, but the deadly slime of his touch still remains."
—JOHN CONSTABLE

"He seems to be the most vulgar-minded genius that ever produced a great effect in literature."
—GEORGE ELIOT

"I cannot think of any other poet of his distinction who might so easily have been an accomplished foreigner writing English." —T. S. ELIOT

"Mad, bad, and dangerous to know"
—LADY CAROLINE LAMB

"The fact is, that first, the Italian women with whom he associates are perhaps the most contemptible of all who exist under the moon—the most ignorant, the most disgusting, the most bigoted; countesses smell so strongly of garlic, that an ordinary Englishman cannot approach them."
—PERCY BYSSHE SHELLEY

"If that man had respected his dinner, he never would have written *Don Juan*."
—WILLIAM MAKEPEACE THACKERAY

"I hate the whole race of them, there never existed a more worthless set than Byron and his friends." —THE DUKE OF WELLINGTON

C

JAMES CAAN
"You can look at De Niro in a film and think, 'Something's eating him.' You look at Caan and think, 'He's eating something . . . pizza?'"
—KATHY HUFFHINES

JAMES M. CAIN
"Everything he writes smells like a billy goat."
—RAYMOND CHANDLER

MARIA CALLAS
"Madame Callas is constitutionally unable to fit into any organization not tailored to her own personality."
—RUDOLF BING

"Normally a tapeworm keeps you thin, but it kept Callas fat. Divas have different metabolisms from the rest of us."
—ANTHONY BURGESS

"She had an extraordinary talent for obtaining publicity at any cost, often on an inartistic level." —DOROTHY KIRSTEN

GLEN CAMPBELL
"Granted, he's very popular as he is, and in my opinion one of the finest singers of our time, but he's been exploited. He's also got lousy taste in song material." —MERLE HAGGARD

EDDIE CANTOR
"One more stand-up joke about me, and I'll knock him down."
—AL JOLSON

AL CAPONE
"It was ironic that a man guilty of inciting hundreds of murders, in some of which he took a personal hand, had to be punished merely for failure to pay taxes on the money he had made by murder."
—HERBERT HOOVER

"I wonder if it is true what I heard about him?—that before retiring each night, he cried like a baby." —WALTER WINCHELL

TRUMAN CAPOTE
"Caposy" —HUMPHREY BOGART

"About as tall as a shotgun, and just as noisy" —TRUMAN CAPOTE

"Say anything you want about me, but you make fun of my picture and you'll regret it the rest of your fat midget life." —JOSHUA LOGAN

"He'd be all right if he took his finger out of his mouth."
—HAROLD ROBBINS

"He is easy to work with, needing only to be stepped on good-naturedly, like the wonderful but bad little boy he is, when he starts to whine." —DAVID O. SELZNICK

"There has to be something wrong with a man who, in *In Cold Blood*, had more empathy for the two killers than he had for the murdered Clutter family . . ." —JACQUELINE SUSANN

"I always said Little Truman had a voice so high it could only be detected by a bat!" —TENNESSEE WILLIAMS
(See also: Jimmy Carter, Norman Mailer)

AL CAPP
"Capp has brought me close to literal nausea a few times on other people's shows with his cast-iron so-called satire."
—DICK CAVETT

THOMAS CARLYLE
"It was very good of God to let Carlyle and Mrs. Carlyle marry one another and so make only two people miserable instead of four."
—SAMUEL BUTLER

CARNAC THE MAGNIFICENT
"All right. So he's not all-knowing. He's borderline."
—ED MACMAHON

JOHNNY CARSON
"I thought he was an ass until I met him."
—MISS LILLIAN CARTER

"To be frank, Carson got right up my nose."
—MARGARET FORWOOD

"The first time we ever worked together many years ago, you were just a snotty guy and it's nice to know you haven't changed."
—BUDDY HACKETT

"That's amazing, at your age, not to use glasses."   —CARL REINER

"He is an anesthetist. In fact, Johnny Carson is Prince Valium."
—MORT SAHL
(See also: Dick Cavett)

KIT CARSON
"The daring deeds of Kit Carson are in no way minimized in a book about them which was written by Kit Carson."
—RICHARD ARMOUR

BILLY CARTER
"Jimmy needs Billy like Van Gogh needs stereo."
—JOHNNY CARSON

"Billy said the extent of my defeat could not have all been attributable to him. I agree. At the most, it may have cost me one or two percentage points."
—JIMMY CARTER

19

"Whenever there's trouble, that's where Billy is. Sometimes when I look at all my children, I say to myself, 'Lillian, you should have stayed a virgin.'" —MISS LILLIAN CARTER

"He and I got to like each other a lot; and I don't even drink beer."
—MIKE DOUGLAS

"Primate of the Decade"
—*Esquire* Dubious Achievement Award, 1980

"Like the girl with the curl in the middle of her forehead, when Billy is good, he is very, very good, and when he is bad he is awful."
—RUTH CARTER STAPLETON

JACK CARTER

(See entry: Milton Berle)

JIMMY CARTER
"The President is delivering a lot of speeches in the Rose Garden—and where he stands it's never grown so good before." —JOEY ADAMS

"I present an engineer's solution. Lay out the problem, lay out the possible solutions and then present a proposed answer. The trouble is that by the time I get to the answer, most people have quit listening."
—JIMMY CARTER

"Carter is prepared to resort to any crime and inflame the entire world." —AYATOLLAH RUHOLLAH KHOMEINI

"Carter, as far as I can tell, is either a character actor or an actor of character." —ALAN JAY LERNER

"I think Jimmy Carter as President is like Truman Capote marrying Dolly Parton. The job is just too big for him." —RICH LITTLE

"His campaign strategy was to remain unclear on all the issues."
—WALTER F. MONDALE

"Carter is incompetent, arrogant, insulated, provincial and unknowing. He is a pious fraud. The pietistic humbug is intolerable."
—DAVID SUSSKIND

"Breaking all records of hypocrisy and lies"
—TASS, the Soviet News Agency
(See also: Walter Mondale)

JIMMY CARTER and RONALD REAGAN
"If I had a thimble, and I poured into it the difference between Reagan and Carter, I would still have room for a double martini."
—STUDS TERKEL

"The one with the fat lips and the one with no lips"
—RAQUEL WELCH

THE CARTER FAMILY
"Carter blood hot, frigid, murky, radiant, mystical, practical, driving—oh, how driving—Carter blood."
—RUTH CARTER STAPLETON

TOM CARVEL
"Do you buy Carvel 'cause you think he's pathetic?"
—ROBERT KLEIN

ROSIE CASALS
"She tried not to, but I really felt sometimes that what she was thinking was, 'I want what you've got so badly that I've got to find a way to somehow destroy you.'"
—BILLIE JEAN KING

JOHNNY CASH
"There was a time when Cash made his stay in the El Paso jail sound like five years in Yuma Prison on piss and punk, though a lawyer named Woodrow Wilson Bean sprung him so quickly Johnny just barely had time to drink a cup of jailhouse coffee."
—LARRY L. KING

QUEEN CATHERINE II OF RUSSIA
"Queen Catherine II, of Russia, imprisoned her hairdresser in an iron cage for three years so that there would be no gossip about the royal dandruff."
—IRVING WALLACE

DICK CAVETT
"Where have you been—living in the subway all your life?"
—TRUMAN CAPOTE

"You speak very good French. In fact, it's so good you could only have learned it in a whorehouse."
—GROUCHO MARX

"You hear it often: Cavett is more intelligent than Johnny Carson and Merv Griffin. It's like saying he is the smartest bear in the zoo."
—MORT SAHL

"I don't think he's as smart as he would like us to believe."
—TOM SNYDER

BENNETT CERF
"I've always told you, Bennett, you're a very nice boy but you're rather stupid."   —GERTRUDE STEIN

CAROL CHANNING
"Carol never just enters a room. Even when she comes out of the bathroom her husband applauds."   —GEORGE BURNS

CHARLIE CHAPLIN
"Charlie Chaplin's genius was in comedy. He has no sense of humor, particularly about himself."   —LITA GREY CHAPLIN

"He was one of the great comedians, and one of the worst appreciators of comedy outside himself and his own genius."
—JAMES THURBER

"I never argued with Chaplin over *Monsieur Verdoux*. What annoys me is that now he pretends that he did not buy this subject from me."
—ORSON WELLES

GERALDINE CHAPLIN
"Although Geraldine has been very successful for so young an actress, I would judge she is not a very soft or a very loving girl."
—PAMELA MASON

PRINCE CHARLES OF ENGLAND
"You're obliged to laugh at his jokes, though personally I don't find him funny."   —CAPTAIN MARK PHILLIPS

G. K. CHESTERTON
"The elephantine capers of an obese mountebank . . ."
—WILLIAM INGE

FREDERIC CHOPIN
"I don't want anyone to admire my pants in a museum."
—FREDERIC CHOPIN

WINSTON CHURCHILL
"Would rather make love to a word than to a woman"
—JOHN BARRYMORE

"Churchill had the habit of breaking the rungs of any ladder he put his foot on."   —LORD BEAVERBROOK

"Winston would go up to his Creator and say he would very much like to meet his son, about Whom he has heard a great deal."
—DAVID LLOYD GEORGE

"About as well suited to our century as a dinosaur"
—JOSEPH GOEBBELS

"The most bloodthirsty or amateurish strategist that history has ever known"
—ADOLF HITLER

"He would, without hesitation, desert a sinking ship."
—CHARLES HOBHOUSE

"I remember him, I don't really know what it was he did, but he was an adorable old man, a really decent old man—a pity he died."
—TWIGGY

THE CLAN [a.k.a. The Rat Pack]
"Membership dues include generally behaving like Mongols from the court of Genghis Khan."
—HEDDA HOPPER

KENNETH CLARK
"My whole life might be described as one long, harmless confidence trick."
—KENNETH CLARK

JEAN COCTEAU

(*See entry:* Gore Vidal)

HARRY COHN
"I don't get ulcers, I give them."
—HARRY COHN

"Thought every actress on the lot owed him sex"
—JOAN CRAWFORD

"Cohn was a man you had to stand in line to dislike."
—HEDDA HOPPER

"Like most roughnecks, he admired gentlemen. Above all, he wanted to be one but had no notion of how to go about it."
—GARSON KANIN

"He had a sense of humor like an open grave." —FRANK SINATRA

ALEXIS CARRINGTON COLBY
"You're a master of disgust, Alexis." —KRYSTLE CARRINGTON

23

SAMUEL TAYLOR COLERIDGE
"Never did I see such apparatus got ready for thinking, and so little thought. He mounts scaffolding, pulleys and tackle, gathers all the tools in the neighbourhood with labour, with noise, demonstration, precept, abuse, and sets—three bricks."   —THOMAS CARLYLE

CHARLES COLLINGWOOD
"Terribly pompous"   —SALLY QUINN

RONALD COLMAN
"He is an excellent director's dummy. He has no personality of his own, only an appearance, and for that reason he is an almost perfect actor for the fictional screen."   —GRAHAM GREENE

JERRY COLONNA

(See entry: Oliver Reed)

CHARLES COLSON
"The rest of us would joke about Colson's ever-expanding empire— the Department of Dirty Tricks, we called it . . ."
          —JEB STUART MAGRUDER

BETTY COMDEN
"She has the face of a very beautiful fox."
          —NATHANIEL BENCHLEY

PERRY COMO
"I'm convinced that his voice comes out of his eyelids."
          —OSCAR LEVANT

JOHN CONNALLY
"I'm sorry to be late. I did my best to hurry, but John Connally had me down at his ranch for a barbecue, and it took me an hour and a half to cut myself down from the spit."   —SPIRO AGNEW

"Nobody ever convincingly imitated Lyndon Johnson except John Connally, and he presumably doesn't mean to."
          —HARRY REASONER

JOSEPH CONRAD
"One of the surest signs of his genius is that women dislike his books."
          —GEORGE ORWELL

ALISTAIR COOKE
"If you stay with me, I'll make you the best light comedian since Seymour Hicks." —CHARLIE CHAPLIN

CALVIN COOLIDGE
"Calvin Coolidge—the greatest man who ever came out of Plymouth Corner, Vermont." —CLARENCE DARROW

"I soon found that he had no liking for many of my water development projects, because they might involve money."
—HERBERT HOOVER

"He looks as if he had been weaned on a pickle."
—ALICE ROOSEVELT LONGWORTH

"He had no ideas but he was not a nuisance."
—H. L. MENCKEN

GERRY COONEY
"I'm not a racist. When I look at Gerry Cooney, I just see a man trying to take my head off." —LARRY HOLMES

JAMES FENIMORE COOPER
"Cooper's wordy prose, overstocked with words of Latin origin, has all the defects and none of the virtues of the style of the period. There is an irritating contrast between the violence of the deeds narrated and the slowness of his pen." —JORGE LUIS BORGES

"And the women he draws from one model don't vary, All sappy as maples and flat as a prairie."
—JAMES RUSSELL LOWELL

"Every time a Cooper person is in peril, and absolute silence is worth four dollars a minute, he is sure to step on a dry twig. There may be a hundred handier things to step on, but that wouldn't satisfy Cooper. Cooper requires him to turn out and find a dry twig; and if he can't do it, go and borrow one." —MARK TWAIN

AARON COPLAND
"If a young man of twenty-three can write a symphony like that, in five years he will be ready to commit murder." —WALTER DAMROSCH

FRANCIS FORD COPPOLA
"Francis Coppola is his own worst enemy. If he directs a little romance, it has to be the biggest, most overdone little romance in movie history." —KENNETH TURAN

HOWARD COSELL

"When you have dinner with him, he broadcasts the meal."
—WOODY ALLEN

"I don't want him to die, but I wish they'd take him off the air."
—MISS LILLIAN CARTER

"He once walked around with a harpoon sticking out of him for two weeks without noticing it."   —DICK CAVETT

"Arrogant, pompous, obnoxious, vain, cruel, persecuting, distasteful, verbose, a show-off. I have been called all of these. Of course, I am."
—HOWARD COSELL

"A cacophony of cockamamie claptrap"   —OSCAR MADISON

"He's the kind of guy who, when he meets someone, says very loudly, 'This must be a great day for you—meeting me!'"   —JOE NAMATH

"He's so nauseatingly gratuitous, going that extra step—including in language, which he cripples while believing he's advancing it."
—MARK RIBOWSKY

"Sportswriter Howard Cosell published a 390-page autobiography in 1973 in which he did not once mention his mother's name."
—LIZ SMITH

"Howard's voice can be heard in every corner of a restaurant, into the kitchen, and out the service door."   —BOB UECKER

(See also: Norman Mailer)

NOEL COWARD

"That staccato voice of his that he shook under the noses of his friends . . ."   —JEAN-PIERRE AUMONT

"Destiny's tot"   —ALEXANDER WOOLLCOTT

JOAN CRAWFORD

"I tried to be a good listener. I decided that was what Joan had wanted after all—not so much a friend as an audience."   —JUNE ALLYSON

"For years, we sent Christmas cards to each other. I'd tell her the latest on my kids, and she'd tell me the latest. Then she would write me a thank-you letter for my card. I couldn't quite carry it that far."
—EVE ARDEN

"Whenever she came to the realization that the men she loved simply didn't love back, she compensated for these emotional setbacks by adopting four children."   —HEDDA HOPPER

"I kept my mouth shut about her for nearly a quarter of a century, but she was a mean, tipsy, powerful, rotten-egg lady."
—MERCEDES McCAMBRIDGE

"How splendid it is that she can still outstare us all."
—MICHAEL REDGRAVE

"She's like that old joke about Philadelphia. First prize, four years with Joan. Second prize, eight." —FRANCHOT TONE

JOAN CRAWFORD and SPENCER TRACY
"I recently saw an old flick starring Joan Crawford and Spencer Tracy in a 'team' picture, and that was a glaring example of what didn't work. Absolutely no chemistry between them." —ROCK HUDSON

WALTER CRONKITE
"The similarities between Rona Barrett and Walter Cronkite are far more interesting than the differences." —ABBIE HOFFMAN

GEORGE CUKOR
"The only man I know who says at ten-thirty, whoever the company may be, 'Time to go to bed.'" —SIMONE SIGNORET

MARY CUNNINGHAM
"She is what most women fear being thought of as."
—GAIL SHEEHY

JANE CURTIN
"That girl is Mussolini in drag." —EMILY LITELLA

TONY CURTIS
"He is, in my book, a passionate amoeba." —DAVID SUSSKIND

GEORGE ARMSTRONG CUSTER
"I don't see how you can make a serious film about a man who seems to have been not only egocentric, but muddleheaded."
—CHARLTON HESTON

D

RICHARD J. DALEY
"Is Mayor Daley still dead?" —PETE BARBUTTI

SALVADOR DALI
"The two qualities that Dali unquestionably possesses are a gift for drawing and an atrocious egoism." —GEORGE ORWELL

"He looks like something he painted. He has long, shiny black hair that keeps falling over his face and he moves around like a cat full of gin." —H. ALLEN SMITH

CHARLES DARWIN
"I have no patience whatever with these gorilla damnifications of humanity." —THOMAS CARLYLE

JOHN DAVIDSON
"John Davidson has no business doing a talk show. He's a singer." —TOM SNYDER

LEONARDO DA VINCI
"I have offended God and mankind because my work didn't reach the quality it should have." —LEONARDO DA VINCI

BETTE DAVIS
"Bette Davis's motion picture career, which began about forty years ago, has been recycled more often than the average rubber tire . . ." —VINCENT CANBY

"I resent her—I don't see how she built a career out of a set of mannerisms instead of real acting ability." —JOAN CRAWFORD

"Who would want to go to bed with her?" —MICHAEL CURTIZ

"I never could stand my face, of course. It was just one of those things." —BETTE DAVIS

"She thought that she was the greatest actress who ever lived." —ERROL FLYNN

"It is as though, whenever she enters any room, she is compelled to use her favorite silver screen expression, 'What a dump.'" —JOSHUA LOGAN

"An explosive little broad with a sharp left" —JACK WARNER

SAMMY DAVIS, JR.
"Dudley [Moore] and Sammy and I were in the same dressing room. It was the first time I'd ever towered over two people in a group of three in my life." —DICK CAVETT

"Sammy can thread a sewing machine while it's going."
—BURT REYNOLDS

JEFFERSON DAVIS
"Ambitious as Lucifer and cold as a lizard"   —SAM HOUSTON

DORIS DAY
"Doris is just about the remotest person I know."
—KIRK DOUGLAS

"You know, J.B. [Jut-Butt], we could play a nice game of bridge on your ass."   —BOB HOPE

"God knows Doris is a strong personality—I used to call her Miss Adamant of 1959."   —ROCK HUDSON

"No one realized that under all those dirndls lurked one of the wildest asses in Hollywood."   —ROSS HUNTER

"My doctor won't let me watch *The Doris Day Show*. I have a family history of diabetes."   —MARVIN KITMAN

"I've been around so long, I knew Doris Day before she was a virgin."
—GROUCHO MARX

"She thinks she doesn't get old. She told me once it was her camera-man who was getting older. She wanted me to fire him."
—JOE PASTERNAK

LARAINE DAY
"Many people found her a strange cold fish of a woman."
—LANA TURNER

JAMES DEAN
"They've brought out from New York another dirty-shirttail actor. If this is the kind of talent they're importing, they can send it right back so far as I'm concerned."   —HEDDA HOPPER

"Dean was sad and sulky, you kept expecting him to cry."
—ELIA KAZAN

SPRAGUE DE CAMP
(*See entry:* Gordon Dickson)

DANIEL DEFOE
"With the one exception of his Moll all Defoe's characters are com-pletely invisible and utterly, not so much as dead, as unalive in the sense that tailors' dummies are unalive."   —FORD MADOX FORD

OLIVIA DE HAVILLAND
"Her horoscope suggests that Olivia would have fared better as an only child."   —JOAN FONTAINE (Olivia's sister)

DOM DELUISE
"One of the world's foremost chickens"   —MIKE DOUGLAS

"A little bit of Dom DeLuise goes a very long way with me."
          —ANDREW SARRIS

CECIL B. DE MILLE
"He wore baldness like an expensive hat, as if it were out of the question for him to have hair like other men."   —GLORIA SWANSON

CATHERINE DENEUVE
"She took the rough with the smooth with apparent serenity. I never noticed that she was quietly sharpening her claws."
          —ROGER VADIM

ROBERT DE NIRO
          (See entry: James Caan)

BO DEREK
"Frankly, I haven't seen anything in which Bo showed she could act."
          —KELLY COLLINS (Bo's sister)

BO and JOHN DEREK
"We hated each other at first. I thought he was mean and he thought I was lazy."   —BO DEREK

JOHN DEREK
"It's only as a pornographer that he's a failure. He's hopeless as a filmmaker too, but probably no one cares."   —DAVID DENBY

VITTORIO DE SICA
"A fine artist, a polished hack, and a flabby whore—not necessarily in that order"   —STANLEY KAUFFMANN

NEIL DIAMOND
"Neil Diamond is unique among pop stars in that he projects not a scintilla of sexual danger . . ."   —RICHARD CORLISS

PRINCESS DIANA OF ENGLAND
"Princess Di took the royal pregnancy test. The peasant died."
          —MAUREEN MURPHY

CHARLES DICKENS
"Of Dickens's style it is impossible to speak in praise."
—ANTHONY TROLLOPE

GORDON DICKSON
"One of those singers with whom science fiction is cursed. Like Sprague De Camp and Poul Anderson, Gordie Dickson has a singing voice of which any walrus would be proud."   —ISAAC ASIMOV

MARLENE DIETRICH
"Marlene Dietrich's legs may be longer, but I have seven grandchildren."   —GLORIA SWANSON

"She has sex, but no particular gender. Her masculinity appeals to women, and her sexuality to men."   —KENNETH TYNAN

PHYLLIS DILLER
"If my jeans could talk they'd plead for mercy."
—PHYLLIS DILLER

"I treasure every moment that I do not see her." —OSCAR LEVANT

"We want to congratulate Phyllis Diller on her award. She has just been named 'Miss Festering Sore.' "   —DON RICKLES

"Phyllis Diller walked into a psychiatrist's office. The psychiatrist took one look at her and said, 'Get under the couch.' "
—HENNY YOUNGMAN

JOHN DILLINGER
"Johnnie's just an ordinary fellow. Of course he goes out and holds up banks and things, but he's really just like any other fellow, aside from that."   —MARY KINDER (his mistress)

JOE DIMAGGIO
"Just one stare from him was worth a thousand words."
—WHITEY FORD

WALT DISNEY
"Disney, of course, has the best casting. If he doesn't like an actor, he just tears him up."   —ALFRED HITCHCOCK

BENJAMIN DISRAELI
"I can understand that Mr. Disraeli should by his novels have instigated many a young man and many a young woman on their way in life,
but I cannot understand that he should have instigated any one to
good." —ANTHONY TROLLOPE

MRS. MARY ANN DISRAELI
"She is an excellent creature, but she never can remember which came
first, the Greeks or the Romans." —BENJAMIN DISRAELI

SAM DONALDSON
"The Ayatollah of the White House press corps"
—RONALD REAGAN

"Word has it that Mr. Carter even said he would willingly bequeath
President Reagan two things—Menachem Begin and Sam Donaldson.
We'll take Begin, but Donaldson . . ." —LARRY SPEAKES

FYODOR DOSTOEVSKI
"In little things he was a sadist towards others, and in bigger things a
sadist towards himself, in fact a masochist, that is to say the mildest,
kindliest, most helpful person possible." —SIGMUND FREUD

KIRK DOUGLAS
"Kirk never makes much of an effort toward anyone else. He's pretty
much wrapped up in himself." —DORIS DAY

HUGH DOWNS
"Hugh Downs even compliments hurricanes!"
—DAVID FRIEDMAN

"If Hugh woke up on Christmas day and found a pile of manure under
the tree, he'd wonder where they were hiding his pony."
—JOE GARAGIOLA

THEODORE DREISER
"He was one of the most churlish, disagreeable men I ever met in my
life, always thinking that everybody was cheating him."
—BENNETT CERF

JOHN DRYDEN
"Read all the prefaces of Dryden,
For these our critics much confide in,
(Tho' merely writ at first for filling
To raise the volume's price, a shilling.)"   —JONATHAN SWIFT

JOHN FOSTER DULLES
"He's the only case of a bull I know who carries his china closet with him."   —WINSTON CHURCHILL

JIMMY DURANTE
"I don't split 'em. When I go to work on an infinitive, I break it up in little pieces."   —JIMMY DURANTE

"The suits he wears are all made by a good custom tailor, but as soon as Jimmy puts on a suit it looks as if he ordered it by mail."
—MAURICE ZOLOTOW

E

CLINT EASTWOOD
"Had I attempted only a fraction of the Clint Eastwood dirty tricks in my films, in my day, I would have been arrested or horsewhipped. Until I quit, most movie fans thought dance hall girls actually danced."
—GENE AUTRY

H.R.H. EDWARD, DUKE OF WINDSOR
"Reputed to have had the smallest reigning penis this side of Napoleon."   —IGOR CASSINI

"The most damning epitath you can compose about Edward—as a Prince, as a King, as a man—is one that all comfortable people should cower from deserving: he was at his best only when the going was good."   —ALISTAIR COOKE

"It wasn't every day that an unemployed polo player became the King of England."   —HARPO MARX

"'You know,' he once said to me with a smile, 'I've got a low IQ.'"
—LILLI PALMER

"He was born to be a salesman. He would be an admirable representative of Rolls-Royce. But an ex-King cannot start selling motor-cars."
—THE DUCHESS OF WINDSOR

JOHN EHRLICHMAN, H. R. HALDEMAN, and HENRY KIS-SINGER
"Known in their prime by such endearments as the Teutonic Trio, the Berlin Wall, and All the King's Krauts."
—DAN RATHER and GARY PAUL GATES

DWIGHT D. EISENHOWER
"When you covered Eisenhower you were always vacationing in Denver, writing stories on how many fish he had caught that day, or what he'd said at the first tee."
—NORA EPHRON

"Eisenhower is acting like a new German Kaiser."
—JOSEPH GOEBBELS

"Proved that you don't even have to have a President"
—HARRY GOLDEN

"John Glenn is running as Eisenhower, Walter Mondale is running as Hubert Humphrey, and Gary Hart is running as John Kennedy."
—EUGENE McCARTHY (1983)

"Good man, wrong job"
—SAM RAYBURN

"He was an amateur in politics; he did not have the slightest idea of the tactics used by the little clique determined to steal the nomination and push him into the Presidency."
—PHYLLIS SCHLAFLY

"You've got to respect [his] clear and forthright opposition to inflation, deflation, fission, fusion and confusion, doubt, doom and gloom, fog and smog."
—ADLAI STEVENSON

T. S. ELIOT
"Every time I read a citation from him I am appalled by the triteness and banality of his utterances."
—HENRY MILLER

"Has arrived at the supreme Eminence among English critics largely through disguising himself as a corpse."
—EZRA POUND

QUEEN ELIZABETH I OF ENGLAND
"She had a membrana on her which made her uncapable of man, though for her delight she tried many, att the coming of Monsieur, there was a French Chirurgion who took in hand to cut it, yett fear stayed her and his death."
—BEN JONSON

QUEEN ELIZABETH II OF ENGLAND
"Elizabeth the Second . . . Elizabeth the Tooth, we call her."
—BETTE MIDLER

"In the early A.M. I was at the foot of her bed eating Rice Krispies."
—DUDLEY MOORE

RALPH WALDO EMERSON
"So perfect a balance there is in his head,
That he talks of things sometimes as if they were dead."
—JAMES RUSSELL LOWELL

"I could readily see in Emerson, not withstanding his merit, a gaping flaw. It was the insinuation that had he lived in those days when the world was made, he might have offered some valuable suggestions."
—HERMAN MELVILLE

FRIEDRICH ENGELS
"The youth of today and of those to come after them would assess the work of the revolution in accordance with values of their own . . . a thousand years from now, all of them, even Marx, Engels, and Lenin, would possibly appear rather ridiculous."   —MAO TSE-TUNG

SAM ERVIN
"The press takes me to task every once in a while, but they have always been very kind, not attributing my hypocrisy to bad motives. They have always attributed it to a lack of mental capacity."
—SAM ERVIN

E.T.
"At first I thought he was gushey, then I got used to him."
—DREW BARRYMORE

FABIAN
"I am 39 and already I can't relate to Fabian."   —LENNY BRUCE

FBI
"Can you picture Christmas at the White House? Santa slides down the chimney and the FBI grabs him for breaking and entering."
—BOB HOPE

DOUGLAS FAIRBANKS
"Douglas had always faced a situation the only way he knew how, by running away from it."   —MARY PICKFORD

35

MORGAN FAIRCHILD
"Created in shop class"   —JAMES BRADY

JERRY FALWELL
"Jerry Falwell says he's going to drive all those people out of office, magazines out of existence, books off library shelves. He's not only an Ayatollah, he's a Savonarola. He has a large hunting list."
                                                           —JAMES MICHENER

FRANCES FARMER
"Hollywood Cinderella Girl has gone back to the ashes on a liquor-slicked highway."   —LOUELLA PARSONS

"The nicest thing I can say about Frances Farmer is that she is unbearable."   —WILLIAM WYLER

KING FAROUK OF EGYPT
"King Farouk was wallowing like a sow in a trough of luxury."
                                                           —WINSTON CHURCHILL

"He came to be entertained, to be fed, to look on, and to belch."
                                                           —ERROL FLYNN

"At times he compelled my mother to smoke a big cigar. My mother didn't like tobacco and he knew it; he seemed to enjoy making her cough."   —OMAR SHARIF

ORVAL FAUBUS
"He had that kind of swarthy and smiling face that is still best described as oily . . ."   —HARRY REASONER

WILLIAM FAULKNER
"For my own part, I can rarely tell whether his characters are making love or playing tennis."   —JOSEPH KRAFT

FARRAH FAWCETT
"I had these teeth when I was eight years old. I had a little head and large teeth. I think that looked very strange." —FARRAH FAWCETT

"Farrah is uniquely suited to play a woman of limited intelligence."
                                              —HARRY and MICHAEL MEDVED,
                                              co-founders of the Golden Turkey Awards

FEDERICO FELLINI
"Fellini never understood female fantasies. Male fantasies yes, but female fantasies no."   —MEL BROOKS

"I mean, you gonna neck with a girl in a five-hundred-seat art house with a Fellini film staring you in the face?"   —JUDITH CRIST

SALLY FIELD
"I certainly don't agree with a friend of mine who says that Miss Field is simply a Mary Tyler Moore someone has stepped on."
—VINCENT CANBY

HENRY FIELDING
"Having no idea of grace, is perpetually disgusting"
—HORACE WALPOLE

W. C. FIELDS
"Mr. Fields, may I borrow your nose for a dim-out lite? Why don't you have your beezer tatooed blue for the duration of the dim-outs?"
—CHARLIE McCARTHY

"My only doubts about him come in bottles."   —MAE WEST
(See also: Mark Hellinger)

EDDIE FISHER
"Never very bright and, emotionally speaking, he wasn't even ready for his bar mitzvah at thirty!"   —RONA BARRETT

"Eddie never loved anybody but himself."   —HEDDA HOPPER
(See also: Elizabeth Taylor)

F. SCOTT FITZGERALD
"Fitzgerald's thin works speak for a thin mind."   —LEON EDEL

"I knew him for two years before he could spell my name; but then it was a long name to spell and perhaps it became harder to spell all of the time . . ."   —ERNEST HEMINGWAY

ZELDA FITZGERALD
"Zelda's face could have landed her in the front line of the Ziegfeld Follies, but she should have kept her bosom strictly under wraps."
—ANITA LOOS

IAN FLEMING
"Definitely a slob"   —MALCOLM MUGGERIDGE

FLICKA
"I wasn't too fond of Flicka. Flicka would stand on my foot."
—RODDY MacDOWALL

37

ERROL FLYNN

"He spent more time on a bar stool, or in court, or in the headlines, or in bed, than anyone I knew."
—GENE AUTRY

"He had no respect for me as an actress because I was a worker at my profession and he wasn't."
—BETTE DAVIS

"The great thing about Errol was you always knew exactly where you stood with him because he *always* let you down." —DAVID NIVEN
(See also: John Barrymore)

JANE FONDA

"Unfortunately, her father's manner was not passed on genetically."
—BARRY GRAY

"Real Women do not want to look like Jane Fonda. Real Women know that pulling your leg up to your head is no way to pose for the cover of a book."
—JOYCE JILLSON,
author of *Real Women Don't Pump Gas*

"We liked her in *Barbarella*."
—RICK MORANIS and DAVE THOMAS

"Humor is not Jane's forte, and she usually fails to grasp a point unless it is stated explicitly."
—ROGER VADIM

"I've known Jane since she was a French housewife."
—GORE VIDAL

PETER FONDA

"Looks as if somehow, on the set of *The Grapes of Wrath,* John Carradine and Henry Fonda had mated."
—PAULINE KAEL

"He talks about LSD like it was a cache of diamonds he suddenly found hidden in a geranium pot."
—REX REED

JOAN FONTAINE

"I think I have become a monomania with her. It is painful to think that her own life is incomplete to such a degree that it's still so keyed to me."
—OLIVIA DE HAVILLAND (Joan's sister)

FORD MADOX FORD

"I had always avoided looking at Ford when I could and I always held my breath when I was near him in a closed room."
—ERNEST HEMINGWAY

"I once told Fordie that if he were placed naked and alone in a room without furniture, I would come back in an hour and find total confusion."　　　　　　　　　　　　　　　　　　　—EZRA POUND

GERALD FORD
"I went to Grand Rapids, Michigan, and found out later that I had called it 'Cedar Rapids.' When Gerald Ford went out castigating me for it, he shouted to the TV cameras that apparently I didn't even know that Michigan was one of the 48 states."　　—JIMMY CARTER

"In *Network,* I patterned the part around Gerald Ford. I mean I pictured Ford in my mind when I played the Midwest business executive running a television network and interested in the bottom line only."
　　　　　　　　　　　　　　　　　　—ROBERT DUVALL

"Jerry Ford is a nice guy, but he played too much football with his helmet off."　　　　　　　　—LYNDON BAINES JOHNSON

"Gerald Ford is the first President of the United States to be elected by a majority of one—and nobody demanded a recount."
　　　　　　　　　　　　　　　　　—LAURENCE J. PETER

GLENN FORD
"If they try to rush me, I always say, 'I've only got one other speed, and it's slower.'"　　　　　　　　　　—GLENN FORD

JOHN FORD
"He had instinctively a beautiful eye for the camera. But he was also an egomaniac."　　　　　　　　　　—HENRY FONDA

JOHN FORSYTHE
"I can't afford, with my limited talents, to bulge. Being a 64-year-old sex symbol is a hell of a weight to carry."　　—JOHN FORSYTHE

"Mr. Soft Voice himself, the incarnation of effortless, gutless acting"
　　　　　　　　　　　　　　　　　—PAULINE KAEL

JOHN FOWLES
"I can't read him at all. Some of his sentences are 150 words long!"
　　　　　　　　　　　　　　　　　　—TOM SEAVER

SIGMUND FREUD
"In my opinion, no self-respecting man ever paid the slightest attention to his dreams."　　　　　　　　—CLEVELAND AMORY

"Nobody can read Freud without realizing that he was the scientific equivalent of another nuisance, George Bernard Shaw."
—ROBERT MAYNARD HUTCHINS

"Sexuality evidently meant more to Freud than to other people."
—CARL JUNG

"In my opinion he made a good job of dumping new loads on us and our consciences."
—HENRY MILLER

"The greatest villain that ever lived, a man worse than Hitler or Stalin."
—TELLY SAVALAS

BETTY FRIEDAN
"I was back in the dressing room and this gal started cussing and arguing something terrible with a guy from a union. I didn't know this woman from Adam. She was running on about women's rights. I said something about 'Isn't it awful what you have to put up with in your own dressing room?' and she smarted off at me."
—LORETTA LYNN

CLARK GABLE
"He used to claim he was very dull in bed."
—EVE ARDEN

"I once declared pontifically that that young man did not have what it takes for a successful career in films."
—CECIL B. DE MILLE

"Listen, he's no Clark Gable at home."
—CAROLE LOMBARD

"His ears made him look like a taxicab with both doors open."
—HOWARD HUGHES

"You can't put this man in a picture. Look at his ears—like a bat!"
—IRVING THALBERG

"Gable's ears stuck out like a couple of wind socks."
—JACK WARNER
(See also: Darryl F. Zanuck)

ZSA ZSA GABOR
"As a graduate of the Zsa Zsa Gabor School of Creative Mathematics, I honestly do not know how old I am."
—ERMA BOMBECK

"Zsa Zsa Gabor has logged millions of miles just walking up and down wedding aisles."
—PHYLLIS DILLER

"I'm a wonderful housekeeper. Every time I get a divorce, I keep the house."   —ZSA ZSA GABOR

"Knew more days on which gifts could be given than appear on any holiday calendar."   —CONRAD HILTON

"Her face is inscrutable, but I can't vouch for the rest of her."
                                                        —OSCAR LEVANT

"Like all women, Zsa Zsa resembles the queen bee, who ultimately kills her mate."   —GEORGE SANDERS

THE GABORS
"Jolie and her brood, Eva, Magda, and Zsa Zsa, have always been the ultimate in playgirls. With over sixteen husbands—or it is more?—between them, to marry into the family you don't have to be crazy, but it helps."   —IGOR CASSINI

MUAMMAR GADDAFI
"Thought his money and his petroleum were more precious than the blood of our martyrs"   —YASSER ARAFAT

"He's the world's principal terrorist and trainer of terrorists."
                                                        —GEORGE BUSH

"Let us tell Gaddafi to take his oil and drink it."
                                                  —THOMAS J. DOWNEY

"As his head bobbed upward and backward, his eyes rolling up to the heavens, he looked like a Monty Python imitation of an Arab weirdo."
                                               —THOMAS GRIFFITH

"Has a split personality, both of them evil."
                                            —GAAFAR AL-NIMEIRI

"I wouldn't believe a word he says if I were you."
                                                —RONALD REAGAN

JOHN KENNETH GALBRAITH
"A common scold"   —JOHN KENNETH GALBRAITH

MAHATMA GANDHI
"In Government circles this sworn enemy of British rule, with his loin cloth, his spinning wheel, his fasting, his public burning of British cloth, his campaign of 'non-cooperation' with the Government of India, was regarded as a sinister if somewhat ludicrous figure."
                                  —H.R.H. EDWARD, DUKE OF WINDSOR

"Half-naked fakir"   —WINSTON CHURCHILL

"Jan. 30, 1948: Gandhi has been assassinated. In my humble opinion, a bloody good thing but far too late."   —NOEL COWARD

JOE GARAGIOLA
"Baseball's George Jessel"   —MAURY ALLEN

GRETA GARBO
"Garbo, Audrey Hepburn, and Mrs. Onassis—all owners of gunboat feet—have made the big, broad, formidable foot absolutely O.K."
                                                      —SHERRY MAGNUS

"I thought you were a fellow I knew from Kansas City."
                                                      —GROUCHO MARX

"Mademoiselle Hamlet"   —ALICE B. TOKLAS

"Taller than I and with even bigger feet . . ."   —RUTH WARRICK

AVA GARDNER
"Ava is a lady of strong passions, something which has mixed merit, one of her passions being rage."   —MICKEY ROONEY

GARFIELD and MORRIS
"American phonies in their loud orange stripes"
                                                      —SIMON TEAKETTLE
    (believed to be the world's oldest self-supporting feline freelancer)

JAMES GARFIELD
"Garfield has shown that he is not possessed of the backbone of an angle-worm."   —ULYSSES S. GRANT

JOHN GARFIELD
"He had a penchant for picking up girls, sometimes two at a time, and a reputation as a demon lover. He died young, in bed, which was understandable."   —LANA TURNER

JUDY GARLAND
"I didn't know her well, but after watching her in action a few times, I didn't want to know her well."   —JOAN CRAWFORD

"Judy's mental attitude may have been pathetic but it turned her into a great bore."   —ANITA LOOS

PAUL GAUGUIN
"Don't talk to me of Gauguin. I'd like to wring the fellow's neck."
—PAUL CEZANNE

GEORGE GERSHWIN
"Tell me, George, if you had to do it over, would you fall in love with yourself again?"
—OSCAR LEVANT

ANDRÉ GIDE
"If you've been married to the greatest writer in the world, you don't remember all the little fellows."
—NORA (MRS. JAMES) JOYCE

W. S. GILBERT
"A misanthrope if ever there was one"
—ALISTAIR COOKE

"I know how good I am, but I do not know how bad I am."
—W. S. GILBERT

VALERY GISCARD D'ESTAING
(See entry: François Mitterand)

WILLIAM EWART GLADSTONE
"For the purpose of recreation he has selected the felling of trees, and we may usefully remark that his amusements, like his politics, are essentially destructive. . . . The forest laments in order that Mr. Gladstone may perspire."
—RANDOLPH CHURCHILL

"Gladstone read Homer for fun, which I thought served him right."
—WINSTON CHURCHILL

"If Gladstone fell into the Thames, that would be a misfortune, and if anybody pulled him out that, I suppose, would be a calamity."
—BENJAMIN DISRAELI

"Despite the fact that at least half the population of England idolized him (irrespective of what the other half thought), a malefactor who ought not to be at large in civilized society."
—AGA KHAN

"Invariably Gladstone earnestly consulted his conscience, and invariably his conscience earnestly gave him the convenient answer."
—BERTRAND RUSSELL

"He speaks to Me as if I was a public meeting."
—QUEEN VICTORIA OF ENGLAND

JACKIE GLEASON

"Jackie cut his finger—it's the first time I ever saw blood with a head on it."
—JOEY ADAMS

"Jackie's consistent, he's got a fat mouth and a fat belly."
—JOE NAMATH

JOHN GLENN

"I told John it wasn't fair for him to take advantage of his hero status as an astronaut. I mentioned this at the unveiling of the portrait showing me invading Italy."
—ROBERT DOLE
(See also: Dwight Eisenhower)

JEAN-LUC GODARD

"Since Godard's films have nothing to say, we could perhaps have ninety minutes of silence instead of each of them." —JOHN SIMON

ARTHUR GODFREY

"He's sweeping the country. But I think Arthur must be doing it with a short-handled broom—he's nearer the dirt than most people."
—FRED ALLEN

"He could sing a little bit and could talk a great deal. He couldn't act."
—MICKEY ROONEY

"By the way, what does he do now?" —ED SULLIVAN

JOSEPH GOEBBELS

"Goebbels was more interested in using his exalted position to blackmail girls into his bed than to transport gold into his vaults."
—ALBERT SPEER

"I had an offer from Joseph Goebbels to work for nothing if he could play himself in *Confessions of a Nazi Spy.*" —JACK WARNER

HERMANN GOERING

"What effeminate behaviour in face of present developments! It is to be hoped that the Fuhrer will succeed in turning Goering into a man again." —JOSEPH GOEBBELS

"Erected to the Headhunter of the Reich by the Wild Animals of Germany, in Gratitude"
—Inscribed on the Goering Monument at Schorfheide
(See also: Martin Bormann)

44

ARTHUR GOLDBERG
"The former everything"   —WILLIAM SAFIRE

HARRY GOLDEN
"High priest of left-wing yahooism" —WILLIAM F. BUCKLEY, JR.

AL GOLDSTEIN
"He is a lovely man when he gets out of that sewer he operates called *Screw.*"   —TOM SNYDER

BARRY GOLDWATER
"You're one of the handsomest men in America. You ought to be in the movies. In fact, I've made just that proposal to Eighteenth Century Fox."   —HUBERT HUMPHREY

"Intellectual pretensions which are sheer mountebank"
                    —NORMAN MAILER

"Goldwater confesses that his grandfather was a Polish peddler. I hope he wasn't peddling the same stuff that his grandson is now."
                    —GROUCHO MARX

SAM GOLDWYN
"In calmer retrospect, I see that much of Goldwyn's curious behavior was due to the fact that he didn't understand the technical side of film-making."   —OTTO PREMINGER

"The trouble, Mr. Goldwyn, is that you are only interested in art, and I am only interested in money."   —GEORGE BERNARD SHAW

RUTH GORDON
"Ruth Gordon plays Lola Pratt, and anyone who looks like that and acts like that must get off the stage."   —HEYWOOD BROUN

"At seventy-four I'm getting minor raves on my looks, but I'm caught in the middle. Who knows what seventy-four looks like? Who cares? But if I'd listened to my friends, I could now lie and say I'm eighty-four. For eighty-four, the way I look is spectacular."
                    —RUTH GORDON

"When she does not have scenes to play in the theatre, she finds it necessary to create them in life."   —GARSON KANIN

MAXIM GORKI
"If I ever meet Gorki, who is said to be an impressive person in real life, or if I ever read one of his books, which are said to be impressive, I shall be awakened doubtless, to a quick sympathy with Russian wastrels. But Gorki on the stage is merely a bore, and a disgusting bore."
—MAX BEERBOHM

ELLIOT GOULD
"Seemed to shock people every time he moved because beads of sweat sprayed out like little diamonds from his neck and arms."
—JOSHUA LOGAN

ROBERT GOULET
"He has effeminate appeal, just like me."   —CASEY STENGEL

SHEILAH GRAHAM
"She is the only member of the press I barred from my sets while I was working. She consistently was rude about my life in her columns."
—BETTE DAVIS

CARY GRANT
"A completely private person, totally reserved, and there is no way into him."   —DORIS DAY

"If no one watched his movies, what would he be?"
—MASON REESE

ULYSSES S. GRANT
"In a picture of the Northern generals, all of whom have identical untidy black whiskers, he is usually the one in the center with his coat unbuttoned."   —RICHARD ARMOUR

GRAHAM GREENE
"If I had worked in a bank I would have dreamed of betraying the trust put in me and running off to South America."   —GRAHAM GREENE

"Should remember that a perception of the vanity of earthly things, though it may be enough to get one into Heaven, is not sufficient equipment for the writing of a novel."   —GEORGE ORWELL

"Though he gives a first impression of being controlled, correct, and British he is actually mad about women. Sex is on his mind all the time."   —OTTO PREMINGER

MERV GRIFFIN
"Double-knit manners are worse than none at all." —*ESQUIRE*
(See also: DICK CAVETT)

ANDREI GROMYKO
"Look at Gromyko—he'd sit two hours on a cake if I ordered him to."
—NIKITA KHRUSHCHEV

BOB GUCCIONE
"Actually quite visual-minded and not entirely stupid"
—GORE VIDAL

ALEC GUINNESS
"Guinness was the most timid actor I'd ever met." —OMAR SHARIF

MRS. GUMM
"My mother was the stage mother of all time. She really was a witch. If I had a stomach ache and didn't want to go on, she'd say, 'Get out on that stage or I'll wrap you around a bedpost.'" —JUDY GARLAND

JOYCE HABER
"She needs open heart surgery and they should go in through her feet." —JULIE ANDREWS

"Joyce Haber of the *Los Angeles Times* once said that the difference between my audience and hers was that mine didn't read. And she was right. They don't read her column, which often duplicates much of my material." —RONA BARRETT

BUDDY HACKETT
"A man who willed his body to science, and science is contesting the will" —RED BUTTONS

ARTHUR HAILEY and HAROLD ROBBINS
"Two of the greatest schlockmeisters in the history of solid waste"
—JOHN SKOW

H. R. HALDEMAN
"Saw no sense in making history if television were not there to broadcast it." —HENRY KISSINGER

"We rationalized that even if he cut you to pieces, at least that proved he was thinking about you."   —JEB STUART MAGRUDER
     (See also entry: John Ehrlichman, H. R. Halderman, and Henry Kissinger)

BILL HALEY
"To me, Bill Haley was a horrible phenomenon."
—GEORGE CARLIN

ALEXANDER HAMILTON
"Now, he was the first Secretary of the Treasury. The reason he was appointed that was because he and Washington were the only men in America at that time who knew how to put their names on a check."
—WILL ROGERS

GEORGE HAMILTON
"He likes to tell me that he barely has bread to put in his mouth. Still, you could throw George in the middle of the ocean and count on him to arrive on shore aboard a yacht."
—BILL HAMILTON (George's brother)

HAMLET
"I cannot identify myself with the prince's problems. Hamlet's mother could have slept with everyone in court and I would still feel indifferent to the hurt it would have inflicted on him."   —CHARLIE CHAPLIN

"The egomaniac part of all time"   —ALEC GUINNESS

HAMLET'S GHOST
"The goddamnedest bore in literature, that pompous ass the ghost"
—JOHN BARRYMORE

MARK HANNA

(See entry: William Buckley)

WARREN G. HARDING
"Harding was not a bad man. He was just a slob."
—ALICE ROOSEVELT LONGWORTH

JEAN HARLOW
"To her, sex had come to be an incessant matter-of-talk that would have bored Messalina."   —ANITA LOOS

"An obstreperously alluring young lady named Jean Harlow of whom not much is likely to be heard"   —ROBERT SHERWOOD

AVERELL HARRIMAN
"Like Coleridge's Ancient Mariner, Mr. Harriman seems to be under some heavy compulsion to justify his failures to anyone who will listen."
—SPIRO AGNEW

PHIL HARRIS
(See entry: George Burns)

RICHARD HARRIS
"He's something of a fuck-up, no question."
—CHARLTON HESTON

"The Real Woman does not like George Segal or Richard Harris. It has nothing to do with being a Real Woman though. No one likes them."
—JOYCE JILLSON,
author of *Real Women Don't Pump Gas*

"He hauls his surly carcass from movie to movie, being dismembered. I'd just as soon wait out his next pictures until he's finished."
—PAULINE KAEL

GEORGE HARRISON
"In his book, which is purportedly this clarity of vision of each song he wrote and its influences, he remembers every two-bit sax player or guitarist he met in subsequent years. I'm not in the book."
—JOHN LENNON

GARY HART
(See entry: Dwight Eisenhower)

MARIETTE HARTLEY
"You have a lot of trouble with men, don't you, Miss Hartley?"
—ALFRED HITCHCOCK

NATHANIEL HAWTHORNE
"Nathaniel Hawthorne's reputation as a writer is not a very pleasing fact, because his writing is not good for anything, and this is a tribute to the man."
—RALPH WALDO EMERSON

HELEN HAYES
"I heartily dislike Miss Hayes."
—JUDITH ANDERSON

"Miss Hayes is not, in my minority opinion, one of the world's most gifted performers."
—TENNESSEE WILLIAMS

SUSAN HAYWARD
"We've become quite accustomed to seeing her expending her pyro-technic talents on lurid and fatuous roles." —BOSLEY CROWTHER

HUGH HEFNER
"If he has done nothing else for American culture, he has given it two of the great lies of the twentieth century: 'I buy it for the fiction' and 'I buy it for the interviews.'" —NORA EPHRON

MARK HELLINGER
"I got Mark Hellinger so drunk last night that it took three bell boys to put me to bed." —W. C. FIELDS

LILLIAN HELLMAN
"She writes like an angel, but she's a dreary bore as spinach is a dreary bore. I say she's spinach and the hellman with her." —TALLULAH BANKHEAD

ERNEST HEMINGWAY
"Always willing to lend a helping hand to the one above him" —F. SCOTT FITZGERALD

"He comes and sits at my feet and praises me. It makes me nervous." —FORD MADOX FORD

"Why don't you go back to bullying Fitzgerald?" —DASHIELL HAMMETT

"Ernest didn't want to be nice. He just wanted to be worshipped." —DOROTHY PARKER

"Hemingway's stupid book comes out and they make a big fuss out of this old man and the stupid dead shark, and who cares?" —HAROLD ROBBINS

"The secret of Ernest Hemingway's big sea catches is that he reels the fish to within twenty yards of his boat, and then machine-guns them." —WALTER WINCHELL
(See also: Thomas Wolfe)

MARILU HENNER
"When we measured heads in eighth grade, mine was the biggest." —MARILU HENNER

KING HENRY VIII OF ENGLAND
"The plain truth is, that he was a most intolerable ruffian, a disgrace to human nature and a blot of blood and grease upon the History of England." —CHARLES DICKENS

"A pig, an ass, a dunghill . . ." —MARTIN LUTHER

PATRICK HENRY
"All tongue, without either head or heart" —THOMAS JEFFERSON

"If George Washington didn't get independence for this country non-violently, and if Patrick Henry didn't come up with a nonviolent statement, and you taught me to look upon them as patriots and heroes, then it's time for you to realize that I have studied your books well . . ." —MALCOLM X

AUDREY HEPBURN
(See entry: Greta Garbo)

KATHARINE HEPBURN
"She ran the whole gamut of emotions from A to B."
—DOROTHY PARKER

LEWIS B. HERSHEY
"A lot of kids don't care for me, but I think most of them are people I don't know." —LEWIS B. HERSHEY

HESIOD
"The learning of many things teacheth not understanding, else would it have taught Hesiod and Pythagoras." —HERACLITUS

HERMAN HESSE
"I found him the kind of writer that college juniors are going ape about. I don't think he adds up to very much in the long run."
—JAMES MICHENER

CHARLTON HESTON
"Scumbag" —ED ASNER

BENNY HILL
"His material is frequently so awful, so barefacedly smutty and silly that you just have to laugh. Or at least to admire his nerve."
—ROBERT MacKENZIE

JOHN W. HINCKLEY, JR.
"The trivialization of love is something I will never forgive him."
—JODIE FOSTER

"The jury should be acquitted on the grounds of insanity."
—JAY LENO

ADOLF HITLER
"Hitler has missed the bus."   —NEVILLE CHAMBERLAIN

"This wicked man Hitler, the repository and embodiment of many forms of soul-destroying hatred, this monstrous product of former wrongs and shame"   —WINSTON CHURCHILL

"A psychopath who somehow found his way from his padded cell to Potsdam"   —MALCOLM MUGGERIDGE

"Adolf Hitler was five feet, six inches tall and weighed 143 pounds. He was renowned for his spell-binding oratory, relations with women and annihilation of a minority people. In his last years, he suffered from insanity and delusions of grandeur. Chairman Mao is taller and heavier."

—National Construction,
The Chinese Communist Quarterly, 1960

"The world is too small to provide adequate living room for both Hitler and God."   —FRANKLIN DELANO ROOSEVELT

"Before this epoch is over, every living human being will have chosen, every living being will have lined up with Hitler or against him, every living human being will either have opposed this onslaught or sup-ported it."   —DOROTHY THOMPSON

"The proper study of mankind is man, and Hitler was a man, however hard that fact may be on the reputation of the human race."
—GEORGE F. WILL

"Didn't you scream laughing at the pansy way Adolf lifted his eyes in that photo in yesterday's *Mirror?*"   —WALTER WINCHELL
(See also: Sigmund Freud, Margaret Thatcher, Alexander Woollcott)

ADOLF HITLER and JOSEPH STALIN
"These men were fantastic and preposterous versions of human beings."   —WILLIAM SAROYAN

JAMES HODGSON
"I don't pay much attention to the Secretary of Labor. After all, when you have a problem with the landlord you don't discuss it with the janitor." —GEORGE MEANY

DUSTIN HOFFMAN
"Better as a woman. If I were him, I'd never get out of drag." —MR. BLACKWELL

OLIVER WENDELL HOLMES
"Had double chins all the way down to his stomach" —MARK TWAIN

HOMER
(See entry: William Gladstone)

HERBERT HOOVER
"A complexion like unrisen dough" —H. L. MENCKEN

"I still favor Hoover for Ex-President." —GEORGE NORRIS

"It was like sitting in a bath of ink to sit in his room." —HENRY STIMSON
(See also: Ronald Reagan)

J. EDGAR HOOVER
"He is a mythical person first thought up by the *Reader's Digest,* and over the years he has become such a legend that no President has dared reveal the truth." —ART BUCHWALD

J. EDGAR HOOVER and CLYDE TOLSON
"I bet they have an orangoutan every night." —LILLIAN HELLMAN

BOB HOPE
"Look, Bob Hope is still about as funny as he ever was. I just never thought Bob Hope was that funny in the first place." —CHEVY CHASE

"A humorless multimillionaire" —STUDS TERKEL

HEDDA HOPPER
"Why don't you leave Hollywood and move to the world?" —MONTGOMERY CLIFT

"Hedda's not a *writer,* I am." —PAMELA MASON

"Hedda Hopper was a dud actress who'd swapped the stage for journalism." —SIMONE SIGNORET

"A gracious battleaxe" —H. ALLEN SMITH

"Downright illiterate" —ED SULLIVAN

"Maybe because she just liked to write nasty stuff and thought the public liked that, Hedda Hopper hated me." —SHELLEY WINTERS

HEDDA HOPPER and LOUELLA PARSONS
"When we cursed them collectively, we referred to them as Lulu Popper." —LILLI PALMER

VLADIMIR HOROWITZ
"Marrying Wanda Toscanini was so typical of him, because he was after a career and adored making money and thought more of himself than anyone else. He had told me that if he was going to get married, he was going to marry someone celebrated." —ARTUR RUBINSTEIN

JOHN HOUSEMAN
"Houseman is an old enemy of mine." —ORSON WELLES

ROCK HUDSON
"I call him Ernie because he's certainly no Rock." —DORIS DAY

"That big, lumpy Rock Hudson" —JAMES DEAN

HOWARD HUGHES
"Old tennis shoes himself" —JIM BACKUS

"He was, from the time we'd occasionally double-dated way back when, the worst dresser I had ever seen." —JACK DEMPSEY

"I was one of the few girls pursued by Howard Hughes who never had an affair with him." —JOAN FONTAINE

"In his heyday, Hughes had boasted of deflowering two hundred virgins in Hollywood (he must have got them all)."
—JIMMY THE GREEK

"One day when he was eating a cookie he offered me a bite. Don't underestimate that. The poor guy's so frightened of germs, it could darn near have been a proposal." —JEAN HARLOW

"It was obvious to me that it wasn't my mind he was after."
—LANA TURNER

HUBERT H. HUMPHREY
"Hubert Humphrey talks so fast that listening to him is like trying to read *Playboy* magazine with your wife turning the pages."
—BARRY GOLDWATER

"Humphrey was Johnson's pet whipping boy, a palace eunuch among eunuchs, politically emasculated by Lyndon Johnson."
—BARBARA HOWAR

"When I want your advice, I'll give it to you."
—LYNDON JOHNSON

"For four years he was a slave to a master who destroys his slaves."
—RICHARD ROVERE

(See also: Dwight Eisenhower, Lyndon Johnson)

TAB HUNTER
"When Mr. Hunter came to Warner Brothers he was about as well-known as a Zulu spear sharpener, and if he was an actor this was a secret known only to him."
—JACK WARNER

BRUCE HURST
"He should be glad he'll be able to tell his grandchildren he once pitched to Reggie Jackson."
—REGGIE JACKSON

ALDOUS HUXLEY
"And do you notice that the more holy he gets, the more his books stink with sex. He cannot get off the subject of flagellating women."
—GEORGE ORWELL

"You could always tell by his conversation which volume of the *Encyclopedia Britannica* he'd been reading. One day it would be Alps, Andes, and Apennines, and the next it would be the Himalayas and the Hippocratic Oath."
—BERTRAND RUSSELL

REGGIE JACKSON
"He'd give you the shirt off his back. Of course, he'd call a press conference to announce it."
—CATFISH HUNTER

"There isn't enough mustard in all America to cover that hot dog."
—DAROLD KNOWLES

"Reggie once said that the only people he can relate to are the writers. That's because they're the only ones who benefit from hearing his crap."　　　　　　　　　　　　　　　　　　　—SPARKY LYLE

"When a streak hitter like Reggie Jackson can get a candy bar named after him, you conclude that the word 'superstar' has been devalued. Or even the word 'candy bar.'"　　　　　　　　　　　—BOB UECKER

MICK JAGGER
(*See entry:* The Rolling Stones)

HENRY JAMES
"If Henry had cared more about a swimming pool and less about his dignity, he might not have spent his career at No. 689 on the best-seller list."　　　　　　　　　　　　　　　　　　—RUSSELL BAKER

"All I recall about Henry James is my mother complaining that he always wanted a lump of sugar broken in two for his tea—and that it really was affectation, as a small knob would do quite well."
　　　　　　　　　　　　　　　　　　—AGATHA CHRISTIE

"A mind so fine that no idea could violate it"　　　—T. S. ELIOT

"Henry James was one of the nicest old ladies I ever met."
　　　　　　　　　　　　　　　　　　—WILLIAM FAULKNER

"I detest Henry James—one of the *worst* writers, abominable, don't you agree?"　　　　　　　　　　　　　　—EDWARD GOREY

"The death of a member of the lower classes could be trusted to give him a good chuckle."　　　　　　　—W. SOMERSET MAUGHAM

"Henry James belonged to a society suffering from the last stages of elephantiasis."　　　　　　　　　　—MARSHAL McLUHAN

"A miserable little snob"　　　　　—THEODORE ROOSEVELT

"Writes fiction as if it were a painful duty"　　—OSCAR WILDE

JESSE JAMES
"The officiating clergyman with much tact avoided dwelling on the life and character of the deceased, and improved the occasion by enlarging upon Jesse's chances of future improvement in Paradise."
　　　　　　　　　—*New York Evening Post* reporting his funeral

THOMAS JEFFERSON
"A slur upon the moral government of the world"
　　　　　　　　　　　　　　　　　—JOHN QUINCY ADAMS

"If Jefferson be elected we may see our wives and daughters the victims of legal prostitution, soberly dishonored, speciously polluted, the outcasts of delicacy and virtue, the loathing of God and man."
—TIMOTHY DWIGHT

"The moral character of Jefferson was repulsive."
—ALEXANDER HAMILTON
(See also: Franklin Roosevelt)

GEORGE JESSEL
"Did you ever catch him at a funeral? It's wonderful. All through the years he makes notes on his friends. He wants to be ready."
—EDDIE CANTOR

"As a young boy he was a precocious moron."   —GROUCHO MARX

"This silly *schmendrick"*   —JACK WARNER

"That son of a bitch started to reminisce when he was eight years old."
—WALTER WINCHELL
(See also: Joe Garagiola)

LYNDON BAINES JOHNSON
"I saw him take some beautiful blue worsted suits and ruin them by putting them on."   —JIM BISHOP

"There is hardly a female reporter in Washington who hasn't danced with President Johnson, and if the President is having trouble finding 50 women for high places in government, he is having no trouble finding 50 women to foxtrot with."   —ART BUCHWALD

"While I am not suggesting that the thirty-sixth President of the United States was a dirty old man, I would not bet the rent money that he was not."   —BARBARA HOWAR

"Johnson had many of the qualities of a true political leader: drive, confidence, great ability, toughness, persistence. But, legend to the contrary notwithstanding, when it came to party politics, he was not good."   —HUBERT H. HUMPHREY

"Sometimes, in sending Vice President Hubert Humphrey off on missions or errands with exhortations to 'get going,' he literally kicked him in the shins. 'Hard,' Humphrey later recalled, pulling up his trouser leg to exhibit the scars to columnist Robert Allen."   —LARRY L. KING

"The country hasn't won a hand since he started to deal."
—RICHARD NIXON

"This Johnson, he's no McKinley." —CARL SANDBURG

"While LBJ is turning out the lights in the White House to save a few dollars—he is also turning out the lights of freedom all over the world by spending $44 million on wheat for the Communist slavemasters. Who's looney now?" —PHYLLIS SCHLAFLY

"I once wrote a short story which wasn't published because of the accusation of hitting President Johnson below the belt. It's hardly my fault if LBJ wears his belt like a crown." —PETER USTINOV

"Johnson's instinct for power is as primordial as a salmon's going upstream to spawn." —THEODORE H. WHITE

(See also: John Connally, Hubert H. Humphrey)

DR. SAMUEL JOHNSON

(See entry: Dorothy Parker)

VIRGINIA JOHNSON

(See entry: William Masters and Virginia Johnson)

GEORGE JONES

"I guess we all handle success in different ways. George Jones ignores it when he can. When he can't he tries to drink it away. When he can't do either one of those, he just walks out on it, even though he knows it'll still come looking for him." —MERLE HAGGARD

"The first time I met George Jones he was in bed with another woman." —TAMMY WYNETTE

TOM JONES

"Tom Jones' pants are so tight, they wear out on the inside." —JOEY ADAMS

BEN JONSON

"I can't read Ben Jonson, especially his comedies. To me he appears to move in a wide sea of glue." —ALFRED, LORD TENNYSON

PAULINE KAEL

"She's an interesting lady, but she doesn't know nearly as much about film as she thinks she does. Even less about acting." —CHARLTON HESTON

KEN KAISER
"He's a lousy umpire. I wish he'd stayed with wrestling and kept that sport messed up instead of baseball."   —JOE ALTOBELLI

"Dr. Strangecall"   —WHITEY HERZOG

"Will chase a manager for unnecessary breathing" —RON LUCIANO

CAROL KANE
"You have to have the stomach for ugliness to admire Carol Kane."
                                                          —JOHN SIMON

GARSON KANIN
"If you were a slave of mine, you know what I'd do? I'd sell you!"
                                                    —SAMUEL GOLDWYN

HAROLD KATZ
"He'd come in after games and put his arm around me and tell me what I should do on the court, like he was trying to coach me. Hey, Harold Katz couldn't be a coach for Wells Fargo."   —DARRYL DAWKINS

ANDY KAUFMAN
"I hear Kaufman is currently trying to get a record company to record him and his grandmother singing a rendition of 'Row, Row, Row Your Boat.' So far, there've been no takers."   —JOHN BLUMENTHAL

"I think that when Andy was born, his father wanted a boy, his mother wanted a girl, and they were both satisfied."   —JERRY LAWLER

"Comedian Andy Kaufman can stop wrestling women and TV execs and start grappling with his clothes. *Taxi*'s Latke dresses like a soggy potato pancake."   —*US*

DIANE KEATON
"In real life, Keaton believes in God. But she also thinks the radio works because there are tiny people inside it."   —WOODY ALLEN

CHRISTINE KEELER
"A twenty-one-gun salute to Miss Christine Keeler (Bang. Bang.)"
                        —*Esquire* Dubious Achievement Award, 1963

EMMETT KELLY

(See entry: Dorothy Kilgallen)

GRACE KELLY
"L'Altesse Frigidaire" [Her Highness Frigidaire]
—BRIGITTE BARDOT

"It isn't the romance that interests Miss Kelly—it's the principality of the thing."
—IRV KUPCINET

EDWARD M. KENNEDY
"Senator McGovern was making a speech. He said, 'Gentlemen, let me tax your memories.' And Ted Kennedy jumped up and said, 'Why haven't we thought of that before!'"
—ROBERT DOLE

"I cannot think of anything in his personal or private life that I admire, and I suppose he feels the same way about me."
—JESSE HELMS

"If I support Ted Kennedy, there would be cruises, jet-set parties and long, lazy summers at Hyannis Port. If I were to support Fritz Mondale, there would be winter in Minnesota. It's a tough choice."
—EDWARD KOCH

"People want Ted Kennedy to be John Kennedy and the people who used to be the Beatles to be the Beatles."
—JOHN LENNON

"If West Germany is the lady sitting next to Teddy Kennedy in a car and the car goes over the bridge, it won't do him any good if he appears at the inquest wearing a neck brace."
—JAMES SCHLESINGER

"Who is he to talk about morals?"
—WILLIAM FRENCH SMITH

JOHN F. KENNEDY
"At one of our meetings he expressed confidence that even if all Mideast oil were shut off, the U.S. had large enough reserves to meet world needs for two years. It was difficult to argue against such deluded self-confidence."
—REZA PAHLAVI, SHAH OF IRAN

"Someone who understands what courage is and admires it, but has not quite the independence to have it."
—ELEANOR ROOSEVELT

"All too often JFK has acted as if he were elected Publisher of the American Press."
—WALTER WINCHELL

ROBERT F. KENNEDY
"I see Robert Kennedy walking through the streets meeting everybody, shaking everybody's hands, and when he gets into office you gonna need a necktie to go and see him."
—MUHAMMAD ALI

"I had seen his face on the bodies of night-time burglars who had been in prison for at least ten years. Robert Kennedy has been in some prison of his character for a long time."   —ELDRIDGE CLEAVER

"He was a parasite who had to work for the government because he wouldn't have known how to make an honest living. He used a knife for a crutch and if it hadn't been for his family he wouldn't have made somebody a good law clerk."   —JIMMY HOFFA

"A young whippersnapper"   —LYNDON JOHNSON

"His body is lean and hard and it is doubtful that he has shed a tear in thirty years."   —FLETCHER KNEBEL

"I just don't like that boy, and I never will. He worked for old Joe McCarthy, you know, and when old Joe was tearing up the Constitution and the country, that boy couldn't say enough for him."
—HARRY S. TRUMAN

THE KENNEDYS
"I am convinced that there was a long-range scheme among the Kennedys to grab the presidency of the United States and keep it in the family for a whole generation."   —JIMMY HOFFA

"The whole Kennedy family, as nearly as I can make out, about all they're interested in is *getting* the power. They don't care a hoot in hell about using it. They're afraid to use it for fear it might not be *popular*."
—HARRY S. TRUMAN

JACK KEROUAC
"That's not writing, that's typing."   —TRUMAN CAPOTE

"Manages to remain true to the spirit of hipster slang while making forays into enemy territory (i.e., the English language) by his simple inability to express anything in words."   —NORMAN PODHORETZ

DEBORAH KERR
"Miss Kerr is a good actress. She is also unreasonably chaste."
—LAURENCE OLIVIER

AYATOLLAH KHOMEINI
"The more he talks, the more he makes himself a laughingstock. I wish the whole world would read his statements to form an impression of this shallow devil."   —SADDAM HUSSEIN

"He leads the people into a daily deification of terrorism."
—REZA PAHLAVI, SHAH OF IRAN

61

NIKITA KHRUSHCHEV
"In the end, we will bury him."   —WILLIAM F. BUCKLEY, JR.

"He may bang his U.N. desk with his shoe, but like every other husband he chickens out when his wife catches him getting bright-eyed about the girls."   —SHIRLEY MACLAINE

"He is a wise peasant bully."   —NORMAN MAILER

"Scheming careerist who's already climbed far beyond his brains and ability"   —JOSEPH STALIN

MRS. NIKITA KHRUSHCHEV
"It would be difficult to find clothes comparable to hers in the waiting room of a New York employment agency for domestic help; in this decadent capitalistic republic, applicants for jobs as laundresses, chambermaids, and cooks usually are far more à la mode than Russia's first lady."   —DOROTHY KILGALLEN

DOROTHY KILGALLEN
"Having your taste criticized by Dorothy Kilgallen is like having your clothes criticized by Emmet Kelly."   —JOHNNY CARSON

ALFRED KINSEY
"He was a boy scout and came very innocently in the country."   —ERROL FLYNN

"I was interviewed by him once and he asked questions like he took it for granted that everyone had fucked everything—from goats to lizards."   —ANTHONY QUINN

NASTASSIA KINSKI
"Keeping in touch with Nastassia Kinski is like trying to find a pearl in fettucine: impossible."   —JODIE FOSTER

"Now Nastassia is passionate about being in movies. Indeed, she has nothing else on her mind, to the point of nausea."   —ROMAN POLANSKI

RUDYARD KIPLING
"Stands for everything in this cankered world which I would wish were otherwise."   —DYLAN THOMAS

HENRY KISSINGER

"I know Mr. Kissinger is a brilliant and learned man and a very scintillating dinner companion. But sometimes even the most brilliant men can be very naive when it comes to women."   —ANN MILLER

"If Moynihan's staff was an Andy Warhol movie, Kissinger's more closely resembled scenes from *Mutiny on the Bounty* . . ."
                              —DAN RATHER and GARY PAUL GATES

"We're civil these days; I generally get along with people out of power."   —WILLIAM SAFIRE (1979)

"Peter Sellers' most deadly deft mimic"   —STUDS TERKEL
(See entry: John Ehrlichman, H. R. Haldeman, and Henry Kissinger)

HORATIO H. KITCHENER
                              (See entry: Wilhelm II of Germany)

HELMUT KOHL
"You always make friendly remarks, Mr. Kohl, but you don't say what you're thinking. Perhaps you don't think at all."
                              —HELMUT SCHMIDT

TED KOPPEL
"He's brilliant. I love him. But he does have funny hair."
                              —STEVE ALLEN

ALAN LADD
"Alan Ladd is hard, bitter and occasionally charming, but he is, after all, a small boy's idea of a tough guy . . ."
                              —RAYMOND CHANDLER

FIORELLO LAGUARDIA
"When I make a mistake, it's a beaut." —FIORELLO LAGUARDIA

HEDY LAMARR
"One evening, when we were driving back from a concert, I braked a little too quickly. Hedy became hysterical, claiming that I had purposely tried to throw her against the windshield because I was jealous of her beauty."   —JEAN-PIERRE AUMONT

DOROTHY LAMOUR
"Dorothy, your hair looks like a cheap wig. Why do you wear it?"
—SAMUEL GOLDWYN

ROD LAVER
"Rod's problem is simple: he's got an ego and he's stubborn, he's too damned stubborn."
—BILLIE JEAN KING

PETER LAWFORD
"If there is anything I think I'd hate as a son-in-law, it's an actor, and if there's anything I think I'd hate worse than an actor as a son-in-law, it's an English actor."
—JOSEPH P. KENNEDY (to Lawford, his future son-in-law)

JERRY LAWLER
"I'd beaten women bigger than him. I really thought I could beat him."
—ANDY KAUFMAN

D. H. LAWRENCE
"The ineptitudes of these awful little love-scenes seem heart-breaking—that a man of such gifts should have lived so long and learned no more about love than that!"
—KATHERINE ANNE PORTER

"Looked like a plaster gnome on a stone toadstool in some suburban garden"
—EDITH SITWELL

"I tried to read his novels. He's impossible. He's pathetic and preposterous. He writes like a sick man."
—GERTRUDE STEIN

TIMOTHY LEARY
"I really think you're full of crap."
—DICK CAVETT

"Creating a group of blissed-out pansies ripe for annihilation . . ."
—ABBIE HOFFMAN

VIVIEN LEIGH
"Everyone talks about the lovely place Vivien had in London. Well, it always smelled like kitty litter, which she kept in the hall."
—JOAN FONTAINE

"She wanted us to be like brother and sister. But, fortunately, occasional incest was allowed."
—LAURENCE OLIVIER

JACK LEMMON
"Lemmon's one of the saddest guys I know."
—WALTER MATTHAU

IVAN LENDL
"All of a sudden Lendl's cool because he's going to hit me? That shows what a classy person he is. We're in two different worlds. That is what *hockey* is trying to get away from." —JOHN McENROE

NIKOLAI LENIN
"I think he was the most evil man—and certainly one of the most imperturbable—I ever met." —BERTRAND RUSSELL

(See also: Friedrich Engels)

JOHN LENNON

(See entry: Yoko Ono)

THE LENNON SISTERS
"I stopped reading movie magazines in the beauty parlor a couple of years ago because I could not accommodate any more information about something called the Lennon Sisters." —NORA EPHRON

DAVID LETTERMAN
"Weird" —NASTASSIA KINSKI

"I'm a smart-ass, and have been for some time."
—DAVID LETTERMAN

"Letterman loves polishing his giant doorknob and planting it on his desk . . ." —JAMES WOLCOTT

OSCAR LEVANT
"I'm a controversial figure: my friends either dislike me or hate me."
—OSCAR LEVANT

"Oscar was a man of principle. He never sponged off anybody he didn't admire." —HARPO MARX

"When Oscar comes on stage he weaves on like a drunk trying to find the rest room. He gropes his way to a chair and slumps in it twitching, scowling, and clutching his heart. 'It might fall out,' he once told me."
—JACK PAAR

"Oscar has mellowed—like an old pistol." —BILLY ROSE

"He was obviously a very tortured man who sprayed his self-loathing on anyone within range." —SHELLEY WINTERS

"There is absolutely nothing wrong with Oscar Levant that a miracle cannot fix." —ALEXANDER WOOLLCOTT

"To autograph seekers he has only three words: 'Go to hell.'"
—MAURICE ZOLOTOW

JERRY LEWIS
"His neorealistic impression of the Japanese male captured all the subtleties of the Japanese physiognomy. The buck-teeth malocclusion was caricatured to surrealistic proportions until the teeth matched the blades that extended from Ben-Hur's chariot." —LENNY BRUCE

"It must be hell to play straight man to an overgrown goof—an unsobering role Dean Martin endured for years with Lewis."
—CAROL FLAKE

"When I was a kid I said to my father one afternoon, 'Daddy, will you take me to the zoo?' He answered, 'If the zoo wants you let them come and get you.'" —JERRY LEWIS

"At some point he said to himself, 'I'm exactly like Chaplin.' From then on nobody could tell him anything. He knew it all."
—DEAN MARTIN

"The great tradition of cheapness and vulgarity will be maintained, even if only by a few stalwarts like Lewis and Sahl."
—JOHN O'HARA

"Pratfalling prince of klutz" —TIME

JOHN L. LEWIS
"John L. Lewis was down in Miami. He wore his seersucker eyebrows." —HENNY YOUNGMAN

SINCLAIR LEWIS
"He was not a personal favorite of mine—I thought he was a difficult man and a habitual drunkard, but I liked his books."
—BENNETT CERF

LIBERACE
"He once visited a funeral parlor and evidently felt at home there; he said the make-up and wardrobe departments were 'just like in a studio.'" —JESSICA MITFORD
(See also: Richard Simmons)

G. GORDON LIDDY
"Once you accept the premise of no-holds-barred intelligence-gathering, G. Gordon Liddy is what you wind up with."
—JEB STUART MAGRUDER

"He's really a pipe-and-slippers kind of guy—lead pipe and hobnail slippers." —MARK RUSSELL

ABRAHAM LINCOLN
"His mind works in the right directions but seldom works clearly and cleanly." —HENRY WARD BEECHER

"The man's appearance, his pedigree, his coarse low jokes and anecdotes, his vulgar similes and his frivolity, are a disgrace to the seat he holds." —JOHN WILKES BOOTH

(See also: Milton Berle)

SONNY LISTON
"He was a cheap and ugly bully without morality, and I had no use for him." —HOWARD COSELL

DAVID LLOYD GEORGE
"He couldn't see a belt without hitting below it." —MARGOT, LADY ASQUITH

GINA LOLLOBRIGIDA
"We disliked each other so intensely that we both considered it useless to make any pretense and did what we could to stay out of each other's way." —MELINA MERCOURI

CAROLE LOMBARD
"Perhaps if she doesn't attempt to act she'll get by." —CHARLES LAUGHTON

HENRY WADSWORTH LONGFELLOW
"Had I accused him, in loud terms, of manifest and continuous plagiarism, I should but have echoed the sentiment of every man of letters in the land beyond the immediate influence of the Longfellow coterie." —EDGAR ALLAN POE

(See also: Ezra Pound)

ALICE ROOSEVELT LONGWORTH
"I can do one of two things. I can be President of the United States or I can control Alice. I cannot possibly do both." —THEODORE ROOSEVELT

SOPHIA LOREN
"Sophia isn't the only woman to have thought her nose was too long. What about Cleopatra's nose?" —OMAR SHARIF

LINDA LOVELACE
"Among the three or four least attractive women I have seen in a pornographic film . . ." —PETER BOGDANOVICH

CLARE BOOTH LUCE
"No woman of our time has gone further with less mental equipment."
—CLIFTON FADIMAN

"What a royal bitch!" —ABBIE HOFFMAN

"Her defeat would be a good thing for this country."
—FRANKLIN DELANO ROOSEVELT

CLARE BOOTH and HENRY LUCE
"Arsenic and Old Luce" —IGOR CASSINI

LORNA LUFT

(See entry: Lee Radziwill)

SID LUFT
"A man with an explosive temper and fists like Virginia hams"
—NATHANIEL BENCHLEY

M

DOUGLAS MacARTHUR
"An obsession for self-glorification and almost no consideration for other men with whom he served" —OMAR BRADLEY

"I studied dramatics under him for twelve years."
—DWIGHT D. EISENHOWER

"I didn't fire him because he was a dumb son of a bitch, although he was, but that's not against the law for generals."
—HARRY S. TRUMAN

ED MacMAHON
"That peculiar fat man who sits beside Mr. Carson for no greater reason, it seems, than to laugh at the scriptwriters' jokes in order to demonstrate to the rest of us that that is what they were intended to be . . ."
—ALAN COREN

GORDON MacRAE

"He'd say, 'You don't have any pimples this week. Have you been making out again?'"

—MEREDITH MacRAE (Gordon's daughter)

THOMAS BABINGTON MACAULAY

"He not only overflowed with learning, but stood in the slop."

—SYDNEY SMITH

JAMES MADISON

"I did not like his looks any better than I like his Administration."

—DANIEL WEBSTER

SAL MAGLIE

"He's got those big evil-looking black eyes. Looks something like Snoopy doing the vulture bit." —JIM BOUTON

"Sal Maglie isn't antisocial, but very seldom did you see him fraternizing. Why? 'I don't want to get to know the other guys too well. I might like them, and then I might not want to throw at them.'"

—JOE GARAGIOLA

JEB STUART MAGRUDER

"Jeb, if you don't take your arm off me I'm going to break it off and beat you to death with it." —G. GORDON LIDDY

NORMAN MAILER

"'Nowadays,' he confesses, 'there are too many times when I no longer give a good goddamn for most of the human race.' It is tempting to observe that nothing would better serve the ends of the goddamn human race than to persuade Mr. Mailer to neglect us."

—WILLIAM F. BUCKLEY, JR.

"A less sturdy intellect than Capote" —ANITA LOOS

"Were it not manifestly unfair to Howard Cosell, that most irritating of broadcasters, it would be tempting to call Norman Mailer the Cosell of American literature." —GENE LYONS

"He's certainly the patron saint of bad journalism." —GORE VIDAL

KARL MALDEN

(See entry: Barbra Streisand)

JAYNE MANSFIELD
"Jayne was wearing a dress which was too tight to walk in. Mickey Hargitay, who was married to her, had to carry her on the set over his head like a suitcase." —TOM EWELL

"She had a very hard tushy." —WALTER MATTHAU

"Miss United Dairies herself" —DAVID NIVEN

MICKEY MANTLE
"Everybody who roomed with Mickey said he took five years off their career." —WHITEY FORD

"Mickey and I are pretty good friends; between us, we've got almost one good pair of legs." —JOE NAMATH

"Mantle thinks I was born at the age of sixty-two and commenced managing immediately." —CASEY STENGEL

CHAIRMAN MAO
(See entry: Adolf Hitler)

FREDERIC MARCH
"He was able to do a very emotional scene with tears in his eyes and pinch my fanny at the same time." —SHELLEY WINTERS

MARINUS
"There is nothing more contemptible than a bald man who pretends to have hair." —MARTIAL

ROGER MARIS
"Rodg always went to first base as though he had sore feet." —JIM BOUTON

PHILIP MARLOWE
"A simple alcoholic vulgarian who never sleeps with his clients while on duty" —RAYMOND CHANDLER

BILLY MARTIN
"Billy is starting to lose his cool. Today he pistol-whipped a pay toilet." —JOHNNY CARSON

"Probably the only person who stays a shorter time in New York than I do is Billy Martin." —MERV GRIFFIN

"Martin made the Yankee clubhouse the most unpleasant place in sport . . ." —MIKE LUPICA

"If somebody would say something in a bar, Billy would have to know why and what they said it for, and it would get into an argument."
—MICKEY MANTLE

DEAN MARTIN
"I wouldn't say Dean has a drinking problem, but his major concern in life is what wine goes with whiskey." —JOEY ADAMS

"Well known as the soberest lush in the business"
—SAMMY DAVIS, JR.

"They wanted me to sit in Dean Martin's lap at the end of a scene. I said no, I wasn't raised to sit in other men's laps, not even for television." —LORETTA LYNN
(See also: George Burns, Jerry Lewis)

STEVE MARTIN
"I wish I was gay. I'd make it with Steve Martin."
—RODNEY DANGERFIELD

"He doesn't own a second change of underwear." —CARL REINER

CHICO MARX
"If there was no action around, he would play solitaire—and bet against himself." —GROUCHO MARX
(See also: The Marx Brothers)

GROUCHO MARX
"If the right situation comes up, he doesn't mind repeating the same joke twenty times in one day." —GEORGE BURNS

"Walked like an arthritic banana." —JACK PAAR
(See also: The Marx Brothers)

GUMMO MARX
"He had about as much equipment for the stage as the average Zulu has for psychiatry." —GROUCHO MARX

KARL MARX
(See entry: Friedrich Engels)

THE MARX BROTHERS
"Nothing but anarchists" —CHARLIE CHAPLIN

"Never saw so much nepotism or such hilarious laughter in one act in my life. The only act I could never follow. In Columbus I told the manager I broke my wrist and quit."　　　　　　　　—W. C. FIELDS

"A perpetual Halloween called the Marx Brothers"　　—BEN HECHT

"Write a show for the Marx Brothers? I'd rather write a show for the Barbary apes."　　　　　　　　—GEORGE S. KAUFMAN

"I never knew what a bicarbonate of soda was until I wrote a Marx Brothers picture."　　　　　　　　—HERMAN J. MANKIEWICZ

WILLIAM MASTERS and VIRGINIA JOHNSON
"My method is basically the same as Masters and Johnson, only they charge thousands of dollars and it's called therapy. I charge fifty dollars and it's called prostitution."　　　　　—XAVIERA HOLLANDER

WALTER MATTHAU
"Looks like a half-melted rubber bulldog"　　　　—JOHN SIMON

VICTOR MATURE
"No picture can hold my interest when the leading man's bust is larger than the leading lady's."　　　　　　　—GROUCHO MARX

ELSA MAXWELL
"And then there's the one about Elsa Maxwell colliding with a Mack truck. The truck lost."　　　　　　　—WALTER WINCHELL

LOUIS B. MAYER
"Put my ashes in a box and tell the messenger to bring them to Louis B. Mayer's office with a farewell message from me. Then, when the messenger gets to Louis' desk, I want him to open the box and blow the ashes in the bastard's face."　　　　　　—B. P. SCHULBERG

"He never was a womanizer. He was so inept in that way."
　　　　　　　—IRENE MAYER SELZNICK (L. B.'s daughter)

"In Hollywood you could make jokes about almost anything, including God and the pope. But you could *not* make jokes about Louis B. Mayer."　　　　　　　　—RUTH WARRICK
　　　　　　　　(*See also:* Jack Warner)

LUCAS McCAIN, THE RIFLEMAN
"This man is a serious psychopath."　　　　　　—JAY LENO

CHARLIE McCARTHY
"I have a little puppy dog and not a tree in the yard. He'll love you."
—W. C. FIELDS

JOSEPH McCARTHY
"The most unlovely character in our political history since Aaron Burr." —DEAN ACHESON

"If Senator McCarthy believed those things when he said them about the Senate Committee then there is a pretty solid ground to say that he ought to be expelled from the Senate for moral incapacity. If he put those things in there honestly believing them to be true, then he has evidently suffered gigantic mental delusions, and it may be argued with much force, that he should be expelled from the Senate for mental difficulty." —SAM ERVIN

"Behaving like a road company Hitler . . ." —ARLENE FRANCIS

"Europeans everywhere were embarrassed and revolted at the spectacle of an America gripped in fear by this vulgar Tartuffe."
—MELINA MERCOURI

"His crawling reflexes, his unnaturally slow and often muddled delivery force quicker minds to function below their normal speeds . . ."
—PETER USTINOV
(See also: Robert Kennedy)

PAT McCORMICK
"I climb him and claim him for America about once a week."
—PAUL WILLIAMS

CARSON McCULLERS
"Artistically gifted and humanly appalling" —GORE VIDAL

JOHN McENROE
"If I cannot hit him with my fists, I will hit him with the balls . . ."
—IVAN LENDL

"I stand around while he complains for half an hour."
—TOMAS SMID

GEORGE McGOVERN
"Doomed to buzz off into the footnotes of history, never having pollinated a single issue." —SPIRO AGNEW

"There really are a great number of people in this country that are a hell of a lot more interested in whether the Dolphins beat the Redskins than they are in whether Nixon or McGovern ends up in the White House."   —GEORGE McGOVERN

"A farmer who wears suede shoes"   —GEORGE MEANY

"So boring he made your skull feel like it was imploding. McGovern said everything in a tired whine."   —TOM WOLFE

ALI McGRAW
"Truly terrible actress, of the nostril school"   —PAULINE KAEL

WILLIAM McKINLEY
"About as much backbone as a chocolate eclair"
                                            —THEODORE ROOSEVELT

"They say he was a nice man, and I'm sorry he got shot. But he was still a damn poor President."
                                            —HARRY S. TRUMAN
                                            (See also: Lyndon Johnson)

ROD McKUEN
"His poetry is not even trash."   —KARL SHAPIRO

STEVE McQUEEN
"You've got to realize that a Steve McQueen performance just naturally lends itself to monotony."   —ROBERT MITCHUM

GEORGE MEANY
"A $100,000-a-year plumber who hasn't fixed a washing machine in 40 years"   —GEORGE McGOVERN

JONAS MEKAS
"His face came to a point in front, and he moved like a bloodhound on the scent."   —ABBIE HOFFMAN

HERMAN MELVILLE
"He is a person of very gentlemanly instincts in every respect, save that he is a little heterodox in the matter of clean linen."
                                            —NATHANIEL HAWTHORNE

H. L. MENCKEN
"H. L. Mencken suffers from the hallucination that he is H. L. Mencken—there is no cure for a disease of that magnitude."
                                            —MAXWELL BODENHEIM

74

"A small man so short in the thighs that when he stood up he seemed smaller than when he was sitting down"   —ALISTAIR COOKE

"Why, the man is an intellectual slob . . . what does he know about stripping?"   —GYPSY ROSE LEE

ADOLPHE MENJOU
"Eyebrows like commas"   —JEAN-PIERRE AUMONT

ETHEL MERMAN
"The walking brass band"   —BROOKS ATKINSON

DAVID MERRICK
"He hates actors, but he paid me the highest compliment. At least I took it as a compliment. He said, 'I don't consider you an actor.'"
     —BRIAN BEDFORD

"He looks like the leading man in a dirty movie."   —MORT SAHL

MESSALINA
(*See entry:* Jean Harlow)

RUSS MEYER
"For Russ Meyer, nothing is obscene as long as it is done in bad taste."   —PAUL D. ZIMMERMAN

BETTE MIDLER
"Second-hand rose after a hurricane"   —MR. BLACKWELL

HENRY MILLER
"When Miller starts talking about Love, not *amour,* I feel like giving him a few francs to go to a brothel . . ."   —ANTHONY BURGESS

"He is a wonderful stylist, and also (as represented by his fictional narrator) a filthy swine."   —GILBERT HIGHET

"The spiritual prophet side of him could produce true enlightenment or fizz and fuzz into the Higher Malarkey."   —JACK KROLL

"A compendium of American sexual neuroses"   —KATE MILLETT

ROGER MILLER
"He thinks it's funny to call people on his portable phone from just outside their motel room doors, then knock. Well, it is funny, but it's a hell of a shock."   —MERLE HAGGARD

JOHN MILTON
"He is perhaps the greatest unread poet the English language has produced."   —RUSSELL BAKER

MARTHA MITCHELL
"A southern charmer one moment, and absolutely impossible the next"   —JEB STUART MAGRUDER

ROBERT MITCHUM
"Standing downwind, Mitchum is probably the sexiest man going today."   —JOAN RIVERS

FRANÇOIS MITTERRAND
"I have been as badly treated by Mitterrand as Sartre was by Giscard."   —SIMONE DE BEAUVOIR

TOM MIX
"They say he rides like part of the horse, but they don't say what part."   —ROBERT E. SHERWOOD

MOLIÈRE
"He should be burned at the stake as a foretaste of the fires of hell."
                    —PIERRE ROULLE

VYACHESLAV MOLOTOV
"My so-called Foreign Minister Molotov, whose brains are just as calloused as his face. He can't even find foreign countries on the map, let alone deal with them."   —JOSEPH STALIN

WALTER MONDALE
"Doesn't hold the popularity; he's connected with Jimmy Carter, who was a colossal flop."   —BARRY GOLDWATER

"Vice President Malaise"   —RONALD REAGAN
                    (See also: Edward M. Kennedy)

JAMES MONROE
"Naturally dull and stupid; extremely illiterate; indecisive to a degree that would be incredible to one who did not know him . . ."
                    —AARON BURR

76

MARILYN MONROE

"There's been an awful lot of crap written about Marilyn Monroe, and there may be an exact psychiatric term for what was wrong with her. I don't know—but truth to tell, I think she was quite mad."
—GEORGE CUKOR

"Marilyn Monroe married a Protestant, a Catholic, and a Jew, and divorced them all; that's what I call brotherhood."
—HARRY GOLDEN

"Copulation was, I'm sure, Marilyn's uncomplicated way of saying thank you . . ." —NUNNALLY JOHNSON

"She exulted in her carnality. As a rising star she posed naked for a calendar. She didn't need the fifty dollars; she just liked the idea."
—WILLIAM MANCHESTER

"You'll not get me with that dame again." —LAURENCE OLIVIER

"She was the worst kind of person—totally helpless."
—VICTORIA PRINCIPAL

"It was like going to the dentist, making a picture with her. It was hell all the time, but after it was all over, it was wonderful."
—BILLY WILDER
(See also: Jane Russell)

VAUGHN MONROE

"Accomplished the impossible: he sang *all* thirty-two bars of a popular song off key." —BARRY GRAY

BERNARD MONTGOMERY

"Would not cease in his efforts to gain personal command of all the land forces and reap all the personal glory for our victory."
—OMAR BRADLEY

DUDLEY MOORE

"Let's face it, Dudley, you are not very long for this earth. You are, in fact, quite short for this earth." —PETER COOK
(See also: Susan Anton and Dudley Moore, Sammy Davis, Jr.)

GEORGE MOORE

"George Moore leads his readers to the latrine and locks them in."
—OSCAR WILDE

MARY TYLER MOORE

(See entry: Sally Field)

HENRY MORGAN
"He wishes everybody were dead, but not in heaven with the angels."
—JAMES THURBER

ROBERT MORLEY
"I have never been willing to sacrifice my appetite on the altar of appearance."
—ROBERT MORLEY

MORRIS

(See entry: Garfield and Morris)

ZERO MOSTEL
"Rolls his eyes on the screen as if he were running a bowling alley in his skull."
—ANDREW SARRIS

DANIEL P. MOYNIHAN

(See entry: Henry Kissinger)

WOLFGANG MOZART
"I write as a sow piddles."
—WOLFGANG MOZART

PAUL MUNI
"The Brothers Warner regarded us as two sides of a coin and did not hesitate to exploit the situation. I disliked Muni and Muni detested me."
—EDWARD G. ROBINSON

THE MUPPETS
"The Muppets have a monopoly on arrogance."
—PATRICE O'SHAUGHNESSY

EDDIE MURPHY
"I love it that despite all his success, Eddie acts like he's twenty-two years old. His life is cars and girls, girls and cars. More cars. More girls."
—JAMIE LEE CURTIS

"The biggest kick is thinking that fifty years from now, people might be watching me on the channel 9 late movie after Joe Franklin, and commenting on how the young Eddie Murphy looked."
—EDDIE MURPHY

GEORGE MURPHY
"Murphy was like an old putrid watchdog, standing point before the master's mansion, bent on seeing to it that nothing got out and nothing got in."   —ELDRIDGE CLEAVER

"Always short on charisma"   —PAULINE KAEL

BILL MURRAY
"He was an incredible slob. He wore shorts, wouldn't bathe for days. He'd go around with six days' growth on his face."
                                                              —LARAINE NEWMAN

EDWARD R. MURROW
"The leader of the cleverest of the jackal pack which is always found at the throat of anyone who dares to expose individual communists and traitors."   —JOSEPH McCARTHY

BENITO MUSSOLINI
"That loud frogmouth"   —W. C. FIELDS

"A displaced Mafia-man."   —MALCOLM MUGGERIDGE

"I am not a man, but an event."   —BENITO MUSSOLINI
                                                              (See also: Jane Curtin)

JOE NAMATH
"The Joe Namaths of the world are meaningless. They come and go, fleeting figures of passing glamour."   —HOWARD COSELL

"Spent four years in high school at the University of Alabama"
                                                              —JACK E. LEONARD
                                                              (See also: Mickey Mantle)

NAPOLEON BONAPARTE
"Old Goldsmith once told me, that when he received a message from the first Buonaparte to attend him at the Tuileries it always gave him a stomachache, and sometimes brought on diarrhoea."
                                                              —BENJAMIN DISRAELI

"Even Napoleon had his Watergate."   —DANNY OZARK

"How often we recall with regret that Napoleon once shot at a magazine editor and missed him and killed a publisher. But we remember with charity that his intentions were good." —MARK TWAIN

(See also: H. R. H. Edward, Duke of Windsor)

NAPOLEON III
"His mind was a kind of extinct sulphur-pit."

—THOMAS CARLYLE

"He is a great unrecognized incapacity." —OTTO VON BISMARCK

MARTINA NAVRATILOVA
"After Wimbledon, Martina said that she wanted to be known as the best woman player ever. What an insult to Billie Jean and me, who have had 10 times better careers." —CHRIS EVERT LLOYD

WILLIE NELSON
"When you talk to him, he looks at you and grins and grins and nods and nods and appears to be the world's best listener, until you realize he is not listening at all." —LARRY L. KING

"It is not officially summer until Willie Nelson puts his hair up in a red bandana." —DAVID LETTERMAN

NERO CLAUDIUS CAESAR DRUSUS GERMANICUS
"Some say that he did, in fact, commit incest with Agrippina every time they rode in the same litter—the state of his clothes when he emerged proved it." —GAIUS SUETONIUS TRANQUILLUS

JEFF NEWMAN
"Jeff Newman ought to be paying three dollars just to watch me hit."

—REGGIE JACKSON

PAUL NEWMAN
"Paul Newman, a lad who resembles Marlon Brando, delivers his lines with the emotional fervor of a Putnam Division conductor announcing local stops." —THE NEW YORKER

"I have often thought that my tombstone might well read: 'Here lies Paul Newman, who died a failure because his eyes suddenly turned brown.'" —PAUL NEWMAN

"While I was very fond of Paul Newman and Peter Sellers, I'd have to say that I would rather kiss a tree trunk. I don't like kissing actors."

—ELKE SOMMER

OLIVIA NEWTON-JOHN
"Miss Smiles herself"   —DAVID DENBY

JACK NICHOLSON
"Looks like a slightly seedy Eagle Scout who is always being stalked by a battalion of slightly aggressive field mice."   —REX REED

LESLIE NIELSEN
"Leslie has high intelligence, and hides it well."
                                                    —ROBERT GOULET

"A ten-year-old dipstick parading around as a genteel fifty-year-old"
                                                    —JERRY ZUCKER

FRIEDRICH NIETZSCHE
"Possessed nothing more than the inner world of his thoughts—which incidentally possessed him more than he it."   —CARL JUNG

WASLAW NIJINSKY
"I'm crazy about insane people."   —TALLULAH BANKHEAD

"The poor boy knew nothing of music . . . complicated and encumbered his dances beyond all reason, thus creating difficulties for the dancers."   —IGOR STRAVINSKY

DAVID NIVEN
"A face that is a cross between two pounds of halibut and an explosion in an old clothes closet. If it isn't mobile, it's dead."
                                                    —DAVID NIVEN

RICHARD NIXON
"In the end, the President turned out to be nearly as devious as the Nixonphobes claimed."   —SPIRO AGNEW

"He always looked impossibly ugly in my eyes."   —ISAAC ASIMOV

"Tricky Dick"   —HELEN GAHAGAN DOUGLAS

"Nixon was the weirdest man ever to live in the White House."
                                                    —H. R. HALDEMAN

"He's like a Spanish horse who runs faster than anyone for the first nine lengths and then turns around and runs backward."
                                                    —LYNDON JOHNSON

"Had matters gone as planned—and the tapes trickled out posthumously—Nixon would have managed the extraordinary feat of committing suicide after his own death."   —HENRY KISSINGER

"I came back at the height of the Watergate hearings because I refused to miss this man's public humiliation."   —JESSICA LANGE

"A featured player who tried to steal the show"
                                                            —ALAN JAY LERNER

"I won't go so far as to say he's insane. I will go so far as to say I find his behavior peculiar."   —GEORGE McGOVERN

"I wish I'd never heard his name."   —MARTHA MITCHELL

"The Nixon Political Principle: If two wrongs don't make a right—try three."   —LAURENCE J. PETER

"The election of 1972 simply goes to prove that America is a land where the lowest, most common man can become president. And he did."   —KIRKPATRICK SALE

"Let's face it, there's something perversely endearing about a man so totally his own worst enemy that even achieving the presidency was merely something he had to do in order to be able to lose it."
                                                            —PAUL SLANSKY

"Are we seriously asked to trust the decision over the hydrogen bomb to Nixon?"   —ADLAI STEVENSON
                                            (See also: George McGovern)

NICK NOLTE
"The star of the hit movie *48 Hrs.* seems to wear his clothes at least that long."   *—US*

KIM NOVAK
"Great parts make great pictures. Great pictures make great parts. This girl has had five hit pictures. If you wanna bring me your wife or your aunt, we'll do the same for them."   —HARRY COHN

RUDOLF NUREYEV
"A rotten dancer"   —EDWARD GOREY

HUGH O'BRIAN
"Wyatt Earp off the set as well as on, six-shooter always poised for action."   —RONA BARRETT

MARGARET O'BRIEN
"If that child had been born in the middle ages, she'd have been burned as a witch."   —LIONEL BARRYMORE

CLIFFORD ODETS
"I don't think writers who cry about not having had a bicycle when they were kiddies are ever going to amount to much."
                                                  —DASHIELL HAMMETT

JOHN O'HARA
"In a perpetual state of just having discovered that it's a lousy world."
                                              —F. SCOTT FITZGERALD

"He likes to admit he is wrong when he is but he doesn't like to be told it."   —JAMES THURBER

OLYMPIC ATHLETES
"There will be outwardly biological women competing in the 23rd Games in Los Angeles next year who, biochemically, have more of the male hormone testosterone pumping illicitly through their veins than the entire male cast of *Saturday Night Fever*."   —DAVID MILLER

ARISTOTLE ONASSIS
"The Greek version of Anthony Quinn"   —TAKI
                                      (See also: Jacqueline Onassis)

CHRISTINA ONASSIS
"Daddy's tanker"   —MR. BLACKWELL

JACQUELINE ONASSIS
"A voice one hears on the radio late at night, dropped softly into the ears by girls who sell soft mattresses, depilatories, or creams to brighten the skin"   —NORMAN MAILER

"When, years later, she married Rumpelstiltskin, I felt like a child discovering, in his father's drawer, the Santa Claus suit."
                                                  —JOYCE MAYNARD

"A woman as avaricious as the Aga Khan"   —TAKI
                                          (See also: Greta Garbo)

TIP O'NEILL
"Not trim enough, nor does he have the outward elegance to cause people to use Latinate words in describing him . . ."
                                                  —JIMMY BRESLIN

YOKO ONO
"She don't suffer fools gladly, even if she's married to him."
—JOHN LENNON

GEORGE ORWELL
"He would not blow his nose without moralising on conditions in the handkerchief industry." —CYRIL CONNOLLY

MARIE OSMOND
"People dwell so much on why Marie won't go to bed with somebody, and they think I'm a little weird because I haven't yet. Like I'm missing a big thing." —MARIE OSMOND (at age 21)

PETER O'TOOLE
"The very stereotype of the ham" —OMAR SHARIF

JACK PAAR
"That guy who made a meteoric disappearance" —FRED ALLEN

"Has gotten himself into awkward situations over the years by taking undue umbrage. Oh well, I suppose it's better than taking Valium."
—STEVE ALLEN

"Paar has a God complex. He thinks he can create performers in six days." —LENNY BRUCE

"The mistake is often made of assuming that the audience of Jack Paar is as loose minded as he is." —WILLIAM F. BUCKLEY, JR.

"Paar wanted you to succeed so much that he would help you to the point of tripping you up." —AL CAPP

"He has a genuine warmth. At the same time he has more reserve and hostility toward an audience than anyone I've ever known. Sometimes I expect him to come out with a whip and a chair." —HUGH DOWNS

"In any other field, Paar might have been dismissed as an immature crybaby." —NORA EPHRON

"TV's most famous terrorist" —MERV GRIFFIN

"Gentleman Jack Paar, America's self-appointed godfather"
—MICKEY ROONEY

"An emotional man who feels the whole world is against him . . ."
—ED SULLIVAN

AL PACINO
"It doesn't even look like the same face anymore. It's pasty, as if he'd vacated it." —PAULINE KAEL

THOMAS PAINE
"A filthy little atheist" —THEODORE ROOSEVELT

JIM PALMER
"Every single gray hair I got, I got from Palmer." —EARL WEAVER

DOROTHY PARKER
"That far off time when Dorothy Parker was alive and bitching . . ."
—QUENTIN CRISP

"Now let's drink to Dorothy Parker. Nothing becomes her so much in life as her nearly leaving it." —ERNEST HEMINGWAY

"I have made it a rule that whenever I say something stupid, I immediately attribute it to Dr. Johnson, Marcus Aurelius or Dorothy Parker."
—GEORGE MIKES

"You see, she is so odd a blend of Little Nell and Lady Macbeth."
—ALEXANDER WOOLLCOTT
(See also: Robert Benchley, Shelley Winters)

LOUELLA PARSONS
"I think Parsons was born with a small pad and pencil in one hand and a shot glass in the other." —JIM BISHOP

"In her own field, where bad writing is as natural and as common as breathing, Louella's stands out like an asthmatic's gasps."
—NUNNALLY JOHNSON

"Louella looked like a very old tadpole." —LILLI PALMER

"Her sneakiest and most valuable asset was looking either stupid or drunk, and getting exclusives in the process." —ROBERT STACK
(See also: Hedda Hopper and Louella Parsons)

DOLLY PARTON
"Why does a country music star wear shirts made from house painters' spattercloths?" *—US*
(See also: Jimmy Carter)

GEORGE S. PATTON
"Megalomaniac"   —OMAR BRADLEY

LUCIANO PAVAROTTI
"I've heard a lot of explanations why he grew heavy—from him and from others—but I think it is very simple: he likes to eat."
—MIRELLA FRENI

"After seeing myself on television for the first time, I lost eighty pounds."   —LUCIANO PAVAROTTI

DREW PEARSON
"America's No. 1 keyhole peeper, muckraker, propaganda-peddling prostitute of the nation's press and radio"   —WILLIAM JENNER

SAM PECKINPAH
"Oh, hell, I can kill five guys and have 'em buried in the time it takes him to kill one."   —HOWARD HAWKS

"Anyone can make a bad movie—only a misguided talent can manage to be terrible."   —ANDREW SARRIS

ROBERT PEEL
"The right hon Gentleman caught the Whigs bathing, and walked away with their clothes."   —BENJAMIN DISRAELI

WESTBROOK PEGLER
"His handling of the language is a beautiful thing to behold, yet his thinking apparatus is warped; nine tenths of the inhabitants of Matteawan are his intellectual betters."   —H. ALLEN SMITH

"The Presstitute"   —WALTER WINCHELL

MARLIN PERKINS
"The Marlin Perkins Law: 'Never make a belt out of a rattlesnake until you're sure it's dead.'"   —PHYLLIS DILLER

JAMES PETERSON [THE PLAYBOY ADVISOR]
"You grew into the job."   —DAVID LETTERMAN

THE PHILADELPHIA EAGLES
"The Philadelphia Eagles sent me a try-out questionnaire. Things can't be that bad, gang."   —LARRY L. KING

PRINCE PHILIP, DUKE OF EDINBURGH
"I am referred to in that splendid language [Urdu] as 'Fella belong Mrs. Queen.'" —PRINCE PHILIP

PABLO PICASSO
"Matisse was as great as his art. That was not the case with Picasso. If you had to be around *him* much, you suffered."
—FRANÇOISE GILOT
(See also: George Balanchine)

MARY PICKFORD
"You're too little and too fat, but I might give you a job."
—D. W. GRIFFITH

FRANKLIN PIERCE
"Pierce was either the worst, or he was the weakest, of all our Presidents." —RALPH WALDO EMERSON

MISS PIGGY
"I think she'd look good with an apple in her mouth, or flying across a football field." —PATRICE O'SHAUGHNESSY

EZIO PINZA
"The odor of his breath was a trial." —LANA TURNER

EDGAR ALLAN POE
"There comes Poe, with his raven, like Barnaby Rudge,
Three fifths of him genius and two fifths sheer fudge."
—JAMES RUSSELL LOWELL
(See also: Jane Austen)

HERCULE POIROT
"Whose appearance impresses one as being rather like that of Humpty Dumpty with a mustache." —JULIAN SYMONS

JAMES K. POLK
"A victim of the use of water as a beverage" —SAM HOUSTON

POMPEY
"The authors of great evils know best how to remove them."
—CATO THE YOUNGER

ALEXANDER POPE
"He hardly drank tea without a stratagem." —SAMUEL JOHNSON

"There are two ways of disliking poetry: one way is to dislike it, the other is to read Pope." —OSCAR WILDE

EZRA POUND
"Pound has spent his life trying to live down a family scandal: —he's Longfellow's grand-nephew." —D. H. LAWRENCE

"I am told you believe yourself to be Napoleon—or is it Mussolini? What a pity you did not choose Buddha." —WYNDHAM LEWIS

"Go swallow a bottle of Coke and let it fiz out of your ears."
—WILLIAM CARLOS WILLIAMS

OTTO PREMINGER
"Otto Preminger was a hard-ass director before anyone knew that Preminger wasn't a skin disease." —JERRY LEWIS

"He's one of that old school of tyrannical directors; he believes that real blood on the actors is better than makeup." —ROBERT STACK

PAULA PRENTISS
"She's Sicilian and has thrown a colander at me from time to time."
—RICHARD BENJAMIN

ELVIS PRESLEY
"He might possibly be classified as an entertainer. Or, perhaps quite as easily as an assignment for a sociologist." —JACK GOULD

"Is it a sausage? It is certainly smooth and damp-looking, but who ever heard of a 172-lb sausage 6 feet tall?" —TIME

"He is the epitome of the unholy marriage of media cowardice and personal no-risking." —RONA BARRETT

"One moment he would be sitting at the table, piddling with his mashed potatoes. The next, he would be head down in the slop."
—ALBERT GOLDMAN

WILLIAM PROXMIRE
"We're getting a little worried about him. We think he's suffering from a military-industrial complex." —SPIRO AGNEW

PYTHAGORAS
(See entry: Hesiod)

FRANK QUILICI
"Minnesota Twin Frank Quilici raised his batting average to .370 by changing his stance so he could see around his nose."
—*Esquire* Dubious Achievement Award (1970)

ANTHONY QUINN
"Needs a personality transplant" —PAULINE KAEL

"You're either going to be one of the best actors around or you're going to be the biggest flop." —FREDERIC MARCH

"'I want to impregnate every woman in the world,' he once told me, though I didn't realize till later how literally he meant it."
—RUTH WARRICK
(See also: Aristotle Onassis)

LEE RADZIWILL
"No matter what she does, she remains, in the eyes of the media and of celebrity watchers, the Lorna Luft of the upper classes." —TAKI

CHARLOTTE RAMPLING
"It's tempting to do crap for a lot of money. She did a lot of crap."
—DIRK BOGARDE

DAN RATHER
"His smile after a light feature in the news looks as if he had just read a cue card saying SMILE." —THOMAS GRIFFITH

"Was not considered a great friend of the Nixon White House"
—HENRY KISSINGER

NANCY REAGAN
"Nancy has this recurring nightmare—she's kidnapped, taken to A & S, and forced to buy dresses right off the rack." —JOEY ADAMS

"I wonder what kind of taste Mrs. Reagan has? Hollywood kind of taste, I suppose." —MISS LILLIAN CARTER

"I think the last book Nancy Reagan read was *Black Beauty.*"
—ROGER STRAUS

RONALD REAGAN

"Jane Wyman seemed more upset with her husband's obsession with politics than I. I tried to make her laugh. 'He'll outgrow it,' I told her. To her it wasn't funny."　　　　　　　　　　　—JUNE ALLYSON

"I don't like him anymore!"　　　　　　　　　　　　　—IDI AMIN

"Ronald Reagan was elected easily, proving that you CAN beat no-body with nobody."　　　　　　　　　　　　　　—HERB CAEN

"It is a mistake, a sign of weakness for an incumbent to blame prob-lems on his predecessor."　　　　　　　　　—JIMMY CARTER

"A punk, a sissy and a coward"　　　　　　—ELDRIDGE CLEAVER

"Ronald Reagan is remarkably fit, but he doesn't cup his hand to his ear as a sunshade."　　　　　　　　　　—SAM DONALDSON

"Contrary to Europeans' general disdain for his intellectual capacity, Ronald Reagan is not a nonentity. True, he is not a hard worker . . ."
　　　　　　　　　　　　　　　　　—ANDRÉ FONTAINE

"Doesn't dye his hair; he's just prematurely orange."
　　　　　　　　　　　　　　　　　—GERALD FORD

"He is silly, he is ignorant."　　　　　　—MUAMMAR GADDAFI

"Ronald Reagan must love poor people, because he's creating so many more of them."　　　　　　　　　—EDWARD M. KENNEDY

"He ticks me off. First of all, he's got hair."　　　　—ED KOCH

"I believe that Ronald Reagan can make this country what it once was—an arctic region covered with ice."　　—STEVE MARTIN

"Herbert Hoover with a smile"　　　　　　　—TIP O'NEILL

"Reagan's is a hairline you normally see only on a child or eunuch. Yet Reagan does not wear a hairpiece and has not been castrated."
　　　　　　　　　—NORMAN ORENTREICH (hair expert)

"In his seventy-third year and too vain to wear a hearing aid"
　　　　　　　　　　　　　　　　　—WILLIAM SAFIRE

"We've got an actor for President, and he's such a bad actor that he gives actors a bad name."　　　　　　　　—ROY SCHEIDER

"The only difference between President Reagan and the rest of the country is that he gets paid for not working." —DAVID STEINBERG

"Reagan will do many things for his country, but be uncomfortable is not one of them."　　　　　　　　　—GEORGE F. WILL

"The biggest alibi artist ever to serve in the White House"
                                                    —JAMES WRIGHT

"Ronnie's the kind of a guy you ask him what time it is, he tells you how they made the watch."   —JANE WYMAN

(See also: Jimmy Carter and Ronald Reagan)

ROBERT REDFORD
"He had asked me to come to Utah for the month to work with him—and he wouldn't give me his phone number."
                                                —WILLIAM GOLDMAN

"(To me) virtually sexless"   —ERICA JONG

"Coping with success is making him cranky."   —REX REED

"He's not six feet tall, either."   —MASON REESE

OLIVER REED
"A dark, stocky man with an unfortunate resemblance to Jerry Colonna"   —ARTHUR SCHLESINGER, JR.

REX REED
"Rex Reed is either at your feet or at your throat."
                                                    —AVA GARDNER

"Eyelashes most women would kill to have"
                                                —MELINA MERCOURI

"Reed is a frustrated little man who wanted to become an actor but couldn't make it."   —OTTO PREMINGER

"Manifestly subliterate"   —JOHN SIMON

MASON REESE
"He thinks he's so smart. He makes me burn up. I'd like to rip him apart."   —RODNEY ALLEN RIPPY

MARY RENAULT
"I'm sure the poor woman meant well but I wish she'd stick to recreating the glory that was Greece and not muck about with dear old modern homos."   —NOEL COWARD

WALTER REUTHER
"You are like a nightingale. It closes its eyes when it sings, and sees nothing and hears nobody but itself."   —NIKITA KHRUSHCHEV

BURT REYNOLDS
"I'm in bed with Burt Reynolds most of the play. Oh, I know it's dirty work, but somebody has to do it." —CAROL BURNETT

"I haven't got a body like his. He hasn't got a body like mine. But that's his problem." —GEORGE BURNS

CECIL RHODES
"I admire him, I frankly confess it; and when his times comes, I shall buy a piece of the rope for a keepsake." —MARK TWAIN

JAMES RODNEY RICHARD
"The biggest feet in baseball" —DAVE WINFIELD

ELLIOT RICHARDSON
"Changed from a transparent toady to a sanctimonious lecturer on morals" —SPIRO AGNEW

DON RICKLES
"The Merchant of Venom" —JAMES BACON

"I don't like the way he closes his act—by apologizing for what he does. It's insincere. A performer who kisses the audience's ass is full of shit." —GEORGE CARLIN

"Somebody has to be Don's friend."

—BOB NEWHART (Don's friend)
(See also: Joan Rivers)

BOBBY RIGGS
"A face like Bugs Bunny" —JIMMY THE GREEK

"I couldn't believe how slow Riggs was. I thought he was faking it."
—BILLIE JEAN KING

MESHULAM RIKLIS
(See entry: Pia Zadora and Meshulam Riklis)

JACK THE RIPPER
"Cut quite a figure in his day." —GROUCHO MARX

JOAN RIVERS
"I saw Joan Rivers in one of those see-through dresses—and nobody wanted to." —JOEY ADAMS

"A depressed area's Don Rickles—only not as pretty."
—ROGER MOORE

"If you get any bigger you're going to become a man."

—DICK SHAWN

"Jealousy is a terrible thing in a woman your age." —BETTY WHITE

FRANK RIZZO

(See entry: Attila the Hun)

HAROLD ROBBINS
"The books I write require twenty percent work, eighty percent disipation."

—HAROLD ROBBINS

"He is able to turn an unplotted, unworkable manuscript into an unplotted and unworkable manuscript with a lot of sex."

—TOM VOLPE

(See also: Arthur Hailey and Harold Robbins)

ORAL ROBERTS
"What do his friends call him? Oral?" —ROBERT KLEIN

FRED ROGERS

(See entry: Richard Simmons)

WILL ROGERS
"Rogers never has been able to discriminate between wit and personalities." —ED SULLIVAN

"About as daring as an early Shirley Temple movie"

—JAMES THURBER

THE ROLLING STONES
"I appreciated their music, but I certainly didn't want to go to bed with Mick Jagger." —BILLIE JEAN KING

MICKEY ROONEY
"Mickey Rooney's favorite exercise is climbing tall people."

—PHYLLIS DILLER

ELEANOR ROOSEVELT
"Public Energy No. 1" —IGOR CASSINI

"It looks like a fight is on between Frank and her to see who will run to be the next President of the United States." —W. C. FIELDS

93

FRANKLIN DELANO ROOSEVELT
"It didn't flatter me to have the squire of Hyde Park come by and speak to me familiarly, as though I were a stable boy and I was supposed to pull my lock and say, 'Aye, aye, sir.'" —DEAN ACHESON

"We didn't know he was going to hang on to that job like the Pope."
—ARCHIE BUNKER

"Preparing the American public for the fact that they have still got to make considerable sacrifices to satisfy his megalomania."
—JOSEPH GOEBBELS

"The Rotarian to end all Rotarians" —MALCOLM MUGGERIDGE

"When it is desired to be called a dictator in the pure classical meaning of the word, Sulla is cited. Sulla appears to us a modest amateur compared with Delano Roosevelt." —BENITO MUSSOLINI

"Thomas Jefferson founded the Democratic Party; Franklin Roosevelt dumbfounded it." —DEWEY SHORT

THEODORE ROOSEVELT
"We bought the s.o.b. but he didn't stay bought."
—HENRY CLAY FRICK

"Now look, that damned cowboy is President of the United States."
—MARK HANNA

"Monstrous embodiment of unprecedented and resounding noise"
—HENRY JAMES

"He has subjugated Wall Street." —JOSEPH PULITZER

"Theodore, if there is one thing more than another for which I admire you, it is your original discovery of the Ten Commandments."
—THOMAS B. REED

"His idea of getting hold of the right end of the stick is to snatch it from the hands of somebody who is using it effectively, and to hit him over the head with it."
—GEORGE BERNARD SHAW

"Merely a helpless and irresponsible coffee mill ground by the hand of God" —MARK TWAIN

KEN ROSEWALL
"Holds the world record for throwing rackets . . ."
—JOHN McENROE

BETSY ROSS

"The only good woman I can recall in history was Betsy Ross. And all she ever made was a flag." —MAE WEST

PORFIRIO RUBIROSA

"He may be the best lover in the world but what do you do the other twenty-two hours of the day?" —ZSA ZSA GABOR

ROSIE RUIZ

"Anyone can enter a marathon, but it takes guts to ride a New York subway." —MELVIN DURSLAG

DAMON RUNYON

"Runyon was a mean-looking little guy, a statue of him would even scare off pigeons." —H. ALLEN SMITH

PRINCE DADO RUSPOLI

"One night, Prince Dado Ruspoli was so stoned that he burned a cigarette hole in my beautiful mink coat, and that damned millionaire prince never paid me for repairing it." —SHELLEY WINTERS

BERTRAND RUSSELL

"One lady whose testimony is to be trusted made the shivering confession that the groping of the noble lord in an automobile conveyed the sensation of 'dry leaves rustling up your thighs.'"

—ALISTAIR COOKE

JANE RUSSELL

"What are the two greatest reasons for Jane Russell's rise to stardom?" —from ad campaign for *The Outlaw*

"We were asked to stick our footprints in wet concrete in front of Grauman's Chinese Theatre, along with the dent left by Jimmy Durante's nose and the print of one of Betty Grable's legs. I suggested that Jane lean over the wet cement so her front would poke holes in it, and that I sit down in it, and we could leave our most important measurements that way, but my idea was vetoed."

—MARILYN MONROE

BABE RUTH

"What a guy—egg-shaped and boisterous, a connoisseur of booze, food and dames" —JACK DEMPSEY

S

SABU, THE ELEPHANT BOY
"He had large, liquid brown eyes filled with a sad innocence that belied the string of knowing blond 'fans' who visited his dressing room, every hour on the hour, sometimes in pairs." —ROBERT STACK

VICTORIA SACKVILLE-WEST
"She resembled Lady Chatterley and her lover rolled into one." —PETER QUENNELL

MARQUIS DE SADE
"If Florence Nightingale had married him, she might have become known as the Lady of the Whip." —MALCOLM MUGGERIDGE

MORT SAHL
"Mort never told me he wanted a better world; he just said he wanted a cowboy suit. If his mother had gotten him a cowboy suit, then maybe Nixon wouldn't have been attacked by him for twenty years." —RICHARD CRENNA
(See also: Jerry Lewis)

YVES SAINT LAURENT
"Why would I or anyone else want to lay me down to sleep with my head on a pillowcase embossed with the signature of Yves Saint Laurent?" —ANDY ROONEY

SOUPY SALES
"Sir Laurence Olivier is a better dramatic actor than Soupy Sales." —PHYLLIS DILLER

PIERRE SALINGER
"He might have had trouble finding an elephant in a telephone booth." —JIMMY HOFFA

CARL SANDBURG
"Give Sandburg a mind, and you perhaps destroy him." —SHERWOOD ANDERSON

"He got us the Australian wood-chopper act, and the fellow who stitches his fingers together with a needle and thread." —ED SULLIVAN

"The cruelest thing that has happened to Lincoln since he was shot by Booth was to fall into the hands of Carl Sandburg."
—EDMUND WILSON

GEORGE SANDERS
"Sanders was such a tight bastard that when Zsa Zsa would ask him for a cigarette, Sanders would charge her three cents."
—JAMES BACON

"You couldn't afford me, but I can afford myself."
—ZSA ZSA GABOR

"I never really thought I would make the grade. And let's face it, I haven't."
—GEORGE SANDERS

SAN DIEGO PADRES
"We play like King Kong one day and like Fay Wray the next."
—TERRY KENNEDY

WILLIAM SAROYAN
"My father never liked me or my sister, and he never liked our mother, either, after an initial infatuation. In fact, he never liked anyone at all after an hour or two."
—ARAM SAROYAN

JEAN-PAUL SARTRE
(*See entry:* François Mitterrand)

THE ENTIRE MALE CAST OF SATURDAY NIGHT FEVER
(*See entry:* Olympic Athletes)

MAXIMILIAN SCHELL
"If a fetchingly cleft chin can be called a performance, Schell can be said to act."
—JOHN SIMON

PHYLLIS SCHLAFLY
"I think her opinions are full of shit."
—TOM SNYDER

JOE SCHMIDT
"A once great player who, as a coach, couldn't inspire a frog"
—HOWARD COSELL

ARNOLD SCHWARZENEGGER
"Has so many muscles that he has to make an appointment to move his fingers."
—PHYLLIS DILLER

WALTER SCOTT
"Did he know how to write English and didn't do it because he didn't want to?"   —MARK TWAIN

THE SECRET SERVICE
"They're afraid if they laugh they'll momentarily close their eyes and they need them for looking around at people who may have guns."
                                    —MIKE DOUGLAS

GEORGE SEGAL
(*See entry:* Richard Harris)

PETER SELLERS
"I would squirm with embarrassment at the demeaning lengths he would stoop to in order to ingratiate himself with the Royal family. It was contemptible."   —BRITT EKLAND
(*See also:* Henry Kissinger, Paul Newman)

DAVID O. SELZNICK
"A typically Hollywood combination of oafishness and sophistication"
                                    —JOHN HOUSEMAN

"He couldn't hire a secretary who could do less than 180 to 200 words a minute dictation—otherwise it would have interrupted his train of thought."   —IRENE MAYER SELZNICK

ERIC SEVAREID
"He is the only news analyst whose shoulders don't fit on the TV screen no matter how far the cameras pull back."
                                    —MARVIN KITMAN

THE SEX PISTOLS
"Seems to me that it was with the Pistols that rock's luck finally ran out."   —STEPHEN KING

PAUL SHAFFER
"Looks like the son James Watt is glad he never had"
                                    —JAMES WOLCOTT

SHAH OF IRAN, REZA PAHLEVI
"The bloodsucker of the century has died at last."
                                    —TEHRAN RADIO

WILLIAM SHAKESPEARE

"I have tried lately to read Shakespeare, and found it so intolerably dull that it nauseated me." —CHARLES DARWIN

"I remember, the players have often mentioned it as an honour to Shakespeare, that in his writing (whatsoever he penn'd) he never blotted out a line. My answer hath been, would he had blotted out a thousand." —BEN JONSON

"Devotedly, passionately heterosexual—perhaps more than normally for an Englishman." —A. L. ROWSE

"For Shakespeare, in the matter of religion, the choice lay between Christianity and nothing. He chose nothing."
—GEORGE SANTAYANA

"The intensity of my impatience with him occasionally reaches such a pitch, that it would positively be a relief to me to dig him up and throw stones at him . . ." —GEORGE BERNARD SHAW

"Shakespeare's hideous stage clowns were the maggots in his apple."
—PETER USTINOV

GEORGE BERNARD SHAW

"He had goat's eyebrows . . . and wintry blue eyes, which reminded me of a dead chicken." —LILLI PALMER

"A blue-rumped ape" —THEODORE ROOSEVELT

"As an iconoclast he was admirable, but as an icon rather less so."
—BERTRAND RUSSELL

"I'm too important to be in an anthology."
—GEORGE BERNARD SHAW

"The more I think you over the more it comes home to me what an unmitigated Middle Victorian ass you are!" —H. G. WELLS

"He hasn't an enemy in the world, and none of his friends like him."
—OSCAR WILDE
(See also: Sigmund Freud, Alexander Woollcott)

NORMA SHEARER

"Slightly cross-eyed, worse than Karen Black . . ."
—JOAN CRAWFORD

SAM SHEPARD

"Harold Pinter is my favorite contemporary playwright. I like Edward Albee and Lanford Wilson. But I would go out of my way to miss Sam Shepard."   —TENNESSEE WILLIAMS

MIMI SHERATON

"I would trust her totally on cottage cheese."   —GAEL GREENE

BROOKE SHIELDS

"She looks like a Halloween trick without the treat."
                                                   —MR. BLACKWELL

JOANNA SHIMKUS

(See entry: Candice Bergen)

TOOTS SHOR

"His idea of great humor was for him to call himself and his pals slobs. I wouldn't argue with the man."   —JOE NAMATH

"Shor has a very loud voice; some of his cronies refer to him as the Loud Adolescent."   —GEORGE PLIMPTON

SARAH SIDDONS

"Damn it, Madame, there is no end to your nose."
                                              —THOMAS GAINSBOROUGH

BEVERLY SILLS

"Isn't Beverly Sills a suburb of Los Angeles?"   —DORRIS KING

RICHARD SIMMONS

"The Liberace of aerobics"   —RICHARD CORLISS

"The grown-up Mr. Rogers"   —JOAN RIVERS

JOHN SIMON

"What a nightmare, to wake up in the morning and realize that you are John Simon."   —GORE VIDAL

FRANK SINATRA

"That show-business despot"   —ISAAC ASIMOV

"I thought he was a fad and wouldn't last."   —GENE AUTRY

"Actually, Frank did me a great favor—he saved me from the disaster our marriage would have been. The truth is he was probably smarter than I: he knew it couldn't work. But the truth also is that he behaved like a complete shit."   —LAUREN BACALL

"When God gave out balls, Frank was definitely first in line!"
—RONA BARRETT

"He's the kind of guy that, when he dies, he's going to heaven and give God a bad time for making him bald." —MARLON BRANDO

"It's hip *not* to ball him." —LENNY BRUCE

"Talk about heart, he's it. Here's a man who last Christmas gave Sammy Davis, Jr., a half bottle of Murine." —RED BUTTONS

"Did you ever try to tell a story to Frank Sinatra? If you do, he's apt to interrupt: 'Is this going to take long?'" —RUTH GORDON

"An exciting sports event is to business what a Sinatra ballad once was to the back seat of a car." —JIMMY THE GREEK

"Hot-tempered, egotistical, extravagant, and moody"
—DOROTHY KILGALLEN

"I can't stand Sinatra, but I like the lyrics of 'My Way.'"
—BILLIE JEAN KING

"When Sinatra dies, they're giving his zipper to the Smithsonian."
—DEAN MARTIN

"His voice is all right if you don't like singing." —LEE MORTIMER

"Make yourself at home, Frank. Hit somebody." —DON RICKLES

"The charm that made him irresistible was often lost in the unpredictable whims of a spoiled child." —ROGER VADIM

"Please, God, don't let us be near when his mood changes, when plates and tables fly through the air, when strong men cower and cringe, and when everybody takes to the cyclone cellars."
—EARL WILSON

GENE SISKEL
"Let's just say that we don't double date." —ROGER EBERT

SPYROS SKOURAS
"The ex-Greek shepherd" —SIMONE SIGNORET

JACLYN SMITH
"The worst tipper in the universe" —SANDRA BERNHARD

KATE SMITH

(*See entries:* Sophie Tucker, Fernando Valenzuela)

STEVE SMITH
"Wearing a shiny light gray suit that looked as if it had to be polished every couple of days. He looked more like an overdressed used-car dealer than the financial wizard of the Kennedy empire."
—HAMILTON JORDAN

DICKIE SMOTHERS
"I always thought Dickie was a wimp and Tommy was all right."
—JOHN LENNON

TOM SNYDER
"Snyder's just a silly ass, and I don't really care what he says about me. He should care what I say about him, and I say he's a silly ass."
—DAVID BRINKLEY

"[David Letterman is] the best thing to happen to late-night TV since Tom Snyder started going to bed earlier."   *—PEOPLE*

ALEKSANDR SOLZHENITSYN
"The Russians displayed uncharacteristic humor in letting this nut come to our shores."   —GORE VIDAL

JOSEPH STALIN
"What a pity that he has turned out to be such a swine."
—WINSTON CHURCHILL

"We never knew, when called to his office, if we'd ever see our families again. You know, people don't do their best work in that atmosphere."   —NIKITA KHRUSHCHEV

"When Stalin sneezed, it was considered by the Russians as a contribution to the science of Marxism-Leninism."   —TITO

"Stalin is the most outstanding mediocrity of the Soviet bureaucracy."
—LEON TROTSKY

"Get plenty of atomic bombs on hand, drop one on Stalin, put the U.N. to work and eventually set up a free world."
—HARRY S. TRUMAN

"Moscow: November 1932. I have been here long enough to learn what the major industry of Soviet Russia is. It is printing pictures of Stalin."   —ALEXANDER WOOLLCOTT
(See also: Sigmund Freud, Hitler and Stalin)

SYLVESTER STALLONE

"*Rocky III*—Surprisingly, he plays a *boxer* in this one."
—JAY LENO

"Sylvester Stallone, who has never been successful in anything but a Rocky movie, will probably have made *Rocky MCMLXXXVIII* by 1989."
—GENE SHALIT

GERTRUDE STEIN

"I'm very proud to be your publisher, Miss Stein, but as I've always told you, I don't understand very much of what you're saying."
—BENNETT CERF

"Literary diarrhea"
—NOEL COWARD

"An old covered wagon"
—F. SCOTT FITZGERALD

"She got to look like a Roman Emperor and that was fine if you liked your women to look like Roman emperors."
—ERNEST HEMINGWAY

"Just an old Roquefort cheese"
—W. SOMERSET MAUGHAM

JOHN STEINBECK

"Hemingway tells me he doesn't think you're all that good a writer."
—HUMPHREY BOGART

GEORGE STEINBRENNER

"George creates an unbearable atmosphere."
—GOOSE GOSSAGE

"Billy Martin was helping the Yankees win titles when Steinbrenner was dreaming of his first polyester suit."
—JEFF GREENFIELD

"I admit it must be tough to want to be a jock and have to settle for being a multi-millionaire."
—LAURENCE SHAMES

"Fuhrer of the Yankees"
—RED SMITH

"I don't barge into the clubhouse like the writers say. When the players come in, I'm there waiting."
—GEORGE STEINBRENNER

"All power people use people. But George uses people worse than all the rest of us."
—FRAN TARKENTON

CASEY STENGEL

"Casey Stengel keeps everybody laughing, but afterwards nobody can remember exactly what he said, if anything."
—JOE GARAGIOLA

"Every time two owners got together with a fountain pen, Casey Stengel was being sold or bought."   —QUENTIN REYNOLDS

"His legs were so lumpy it looked as though he were smuggling walnuts in his stockings."   —BOB UECKER

(See also: Robert Goulet)

McLEAN STEVENSON
"McLean Stevenson showed as unprofessional conduct as I have ever seen in more than fifty years in the business."   —JACKIE COOPER

ROD STEWART
"Soddy was my pet name for Rod. There were times when he was such a sod even in his most charming moods."   —BRITT EKLAND

DAVID STOCKMAN
"A pathological finagler"   —FRITZ HOLLINGS

LEE STRASBERG
"My opinion of his school is that it did more harm than good to his students . . ."   —LAURENCE OLIVIER

MERYL STREEP
"Her nose: that red thin sharp snout—it reminds you of an anteater."   —TRUMAN CAPOTE

"The only problem I have with Meryl Streep is pronouncing her name."   —MARK RUSSELL

BARBRA STREISAND
"We are dining tonight at the Russian Tea Room. Hope to catch a glimpse of Barbra Streisand or Karl Malden or anyone else with a slightly odd nose."   —MICHAEL PALIN

"To know her is not necessarily to love her."   —REX REED

SULLA

(See entry: Franklin Delano Roosevelt)

ARTHUR SULLIVAN
"He is like a man who sits on a stove and then complains that his backside is burning."   —W. S. GILBERT

ED SULLIVAN
"What does Sullivan do? He points at people. Rub meat on actors and dogs will do the same." —FRED ALLEN

"He'll be dynamic. He's going to walk and everything." —JACK BENNY

"Ed Sullivan has introduced me as Jack Carson, John Crater, John Kerr and Carson McCullers." —JACK CARSON

"While he doesn't sing, dance or tell jokes, he does them equally well." —BING CROSBY

"Ed Sullivan was on television two years before it was invented." —BOB HOPE

"More incoherent, more emotional and more nutty than I am." —JACK PAAR

"Sick, sick, sick" —FRANK SINATRA

"He got where he is not by having a personality but by having no personality . . ." —HARRIET VAN HORNE

"In Africa the cannibals adored him. They thought he was some new kind of frozen food." —HENNY YOUNGMAN

JACQUELINE SUSANN
"A truckdriver in drag" —TRUMAN CAPOTE

DAVID SUSSKIND
"Television's worst C-E-N-S-O-R" —ABBIE HOFFMAN

DONALD SUTHERLAND
"I knew I was a homely kid. They don't call you Goofus and Dumbo for nothing." —DONALD SUTHERLAND

GLORIA SWANSON
"Queen Gloria Swanson who knocked people about like bowling pins" —LOUISE BROOKS

LORETTA SWIT
"Became totally undirectable" —JACKIE COOPER

FRAN TARKENTON
"An ego run amok" —MARK RIBOWSKY

105

DR. HERBERT TARNOWER
"A creep of cosmic dimensions"   —BETH FALLON

ELIZABETH TAYLOR
"A perfect camera subject like Elizabeth Taylor let herself become un-photographable."   —CECIL BEATON

"Not one movie star has worse taste."   —MR. BLACKWELL

"She has a double chin and an overdeveloped chest and she's rather short in the legs. So I can hardly describe her as the most beautiful creature I've ever seen."   —RICHARD BURTON

"Gotta get rollers on that lady."   —JOHNNY CARSON

"Never fails to try to con my diamond rings from me."
                    —SAMMY DAVIS, JR.

"Any man who hasn't fantasized about Elizabeth Taylor is either a homosexual or an agent."   —BUDDY HACKETT

"By the time the asp had gotten to Liz Taylor in *Cleopatra,* the studio had lost more than Eddie Fisher."   —BOB HOPE

"From ingenue-goddess, she went right over the hill."
                    —PAULINE KAEL

"She's not acting at all. She simply doesn't know how."
                    —WALTER KERR

"Elizabeth Taylor should get a divorce and settle down."
                    —JACK PAAR

"Marrying her is like trying to flag down the Twentieth Century Limited with a Zippo lighter."   —RALPH PEARL

"Is she fat? Her favorite food is seconds."   —JOAN RIVERS

"Elizabeth and I have a lot in common. We both like jewelry. It's just a question of size. We also both have this thing about actors. And again, it's just a question of size."   —DINAH SHORE

"I am wonderful at playing bitches."   —ELIZABETH TAYLOR

JAMES TAYLOR
"James was the kind of person you looked at and wanted to save. We went to live on Martha's Vineyard, and when I arrived at his house, I found two years' worth of unopened mail stacked up to the ceiling."
                    —CARLY SIMON

RENATA TEBALDI
"Dimples of iron"   —RUDOLF BING

SHIRLEY TEMPLE
"A 50-year-old midget"   —MAE WEST

ALFRED, LORD TENNYSON
"He had an almost theatrically pink complexion and two red spots on his cheeks. I think he used makeup."   —BERTRAND RUSSELL

MARGARET THATCHER
"The industrial destruction she has inflicted upon this country is even worse than Hitler's bombings."   —MICHAEL FOOT

"Turned the Tory Party into her personal dictatorship"
                                                     —DENIS HEALEY

"If I were married to her, I'd be sure to have dinner ready when she got home."   —GEORGE SHULTZ

DYLAN THOMAS
"A Welsh demagogic masturbator who failed to pay his bills"
                                                     —ROBERT GRAVES

HENRY DAVID THOREAU
"He was worse than provincial—he was parochial."
                                                     —HENRY JAMES, JR.

CHARLENE TILTON
"A Victorian lampshade holding her breasts"   —MR. BLACKWELL

CLYDE TOLSON
                    (See entry: J. Edgar Hoover and Clyde Tolson)
LEO TOLSTOI
"The poor chap has no technique."   —CLIFTON FADIMAN
                              (See also: Honoré de Balzac)

SPENCER TRACY
                    (See entry: Joan Crawford and Spencer Tracy)

JOHN TRAVOLTA
"He may become a Dead End Kid of the 1970s, and for an actor as ambitious as Travolta is, that could *be* a dead end." —GENE SHALIT

TRESSIE DOLLS
                              (See entry: Barbie Dolls)

CALVIN TRILLIN
"That droll potato"   —JAMES WOLCOTT

PIERRE TRUDEAU
"Has very negative feelings about television. He tried to give me the argument that the brain can actually be damaged by the waves."
                                                      —MARGARET TRUDEAU

HARRY S. TRUMAN
"Proved that just about anyone could be president"
                                                      —HARRY GOLDEN

"Truman's technique is never to deal with problems, but only with the excellent results that would be achieved if the problems had been solved."   —WALTER LIPPMANN

"Harry Truman. A study in failure."
                                 —headline, England's *Manchester Guardian*

"Surely the most pathetically inadequate figure ever placed in a position of exercising so great authority to so little effect."
                                                      —MALCOLM MUGGERIDGE

SOPHIE TUCKER
"Outweighed Kate Smith by 100 lbs. troy weight"   —W. C. FIELDS

MARK TWAIN
"Whenever I want to write about a foreign country, I read Twain to be sure that I don't do the things he did. . . . I find it repulsive."
                                                      —JAMES MICHENER

TWIGGY and TOMMY TUNE
"I've never had a partner I matched so well. Our only problem is that we're so skinny our bones clank when we dance."   —TOMMY TUNE

KENNETH TYNAN
"Carried on the great and lucrative English tradition of charging the United States a handsome sum of money for telling us how ugly we are."   —WILLIAM F. BUCKLEY, JR.

𝒰

FELIX UNGER
"A noble drone"   —HOWARD COSELL

JOHN UPDIKE
"Has nothing to say"   —JOHN ALDRIDGE

"He writes essentially nineteenth-century novels. He's irrelevant."
—LESLIE FIEDLER

V

ROGER VADIM
"He snored in his sleep and walked about the flat half the day in his suspenders, and worst of all, he had become more of a brother than a lover."   —BRIGITTE BARDOT

FERNANDO VALENZUELA
"Watching Fernando Valenzuela force himself into a Dodger uniform is like seeing Kate Smith struggling to fit into a pair of Brooke Shields' designer jeans."   —H. G. REZA

MARTIN VAN BUREN
"He is an artful, cunning, intriguing, selfish, speculating lawyer, who, by holding lucrative offices for more than half of his life, has contrived to amass a princely fortune, and is now seeking the Presidency, principally for sordid gain, and to gratify the most selfish ambition."
—DAVY CROCKETT

COMMODORE VANDERBILT
"He really treated his daughters very badly. I imagine he was the supreme male chauvinist."   —GLORIA VANDERBILT

GLORIA VANDERBILT
"Frankly, I wouldn't want Gloria's name on my tail, and I'm surprised she'd want it there either."   —ANDY ROONEY

HARRIET VAN HORNE
"Dear Miss Van Horne, You bitch. Sincerely, Ed Sullivan."
—ED SULLIVAN

SID VICIOUS
"Sid Vicious died for what? So that we might rock? I mean, it's garbage, you know."   —JOHN LENNON

"Luridly putrid"   —TOM WOLFE

QUEEN VICTORIA OF ENGLAND
"A tea cozy, I think, would describe her adequately."
                                        —BERTRAND RUSSELL

"Nowadays, a parlour maid as ignorant as Queen Victoria was when she came to the throne, would be classed as mentally defective."
                                        —GEORGE BERNARD SHAW

"If this is the way Queen Victoria treats her convicts, she doesn't deserve to have any."   —OSCAR WILDE

GORE VIDAL
"Gore Vidal, who I feel doesn't think any of us, of any age, are qualified to vote. Nevertheless, I'm sure he would insist on our right to do so."   —MIKE DOUGLAS

"It says a lot about the United States of America that such a foreign object as Gore Vidal can run for the Senate."   —JANE FONDA

"Gore Vidal must be the nastiest man in the world."
                                        —LYNDA BIRD JOHNSON

"Vidal gets more literary mileage out of his sex life than anyone since Oscar Wilde and Jean Cocteau."   —ALFRED KAZIN

"I've had to smell your works from time to time, and that has helped me to become an expert on intellectual pollution."
                                        —NORMAN MAILER

WERNHER VON BRAUN
"He had worked under Hitler and would have won the war for the Nazis if he could."   —ISAAC ASIMOV

ERICH VON STROHEIM
"I'm not a Prussian. I'm Austrian. It's like calling an Englishman Irish. And my head isn't bullet-shaped. I've seen bullets."
                                        —ERICH VON STROHEIM

W

RICHARD WAGNER
"Is Wagner a human being at all? Is he not rather a disease?"
                                        —FRIEDRICH NIETZSCHE

"One can't judge Wagner's opera *Lohengrin* after a first hearing, and I certainly don't intend hearing it a second time."
—GIOACCHINO ROSSINI

"Wagner's music is better than it sounds."   —MARK TWAIN

"I am quick to agree with the feeling of Nietzsche that the thundering, melodious balderdash of Wagner was the most addling experience imaginable for the German intellect."   —KURT VONNEGUT, JR.
(See also: Bertolt Brecht)

PORTER WAGONER
"He's helped a lot of people in country music get their start, but I'll bet I'm the only one he's ever helped by not helping."
—TAMMY WYNETTE

GEORGE WALLACE
"Bigger eyes for women than ears"   —BARBARA HOWAR

"A fourth-rate regional demagogue"   —DANIEL P. MOYNIHAN

MIKE WALLACE
"I don't like him very much and I'm sure he doesn't like me."
—PETE MARTIN

"How would Mike Wallace like it if he were to come on a show and we forever dredged up the fact that he used to sell cigarettes on TV? Or that he did quiz shows?"   —TOM SNYDER

RAOUL WALSH
"To Raoul Walsh a tender love scene is burning down a whorehouse."
—JACK WARNER

BARBARA WALTERS
"Strikes me as such a ball-cutting lady"   —CHARLTON HESTON

"I never heard of her till she got all that money."
—REGGIE JACKSON

"The all-time Olympics award for the dumbest question on TV has to go to Barbara Walters."   —JACK PAAR

"My mummy can't drive a car, you know. My mummy can't fix a fuse. My mummy burns the meat loaf. Come to think of it, my mummy really can't do anything but talk."   —JACQUELINE WALTERS

"A hyena in syrup"   —YEVGENY YEVTUSHENKO

ANDY WARHOL
"Warhol's output is of no value, but great interest."

—DAVID DENBY

"The highly publicized arrival of the Andy Warhol robot, produced at a factory in Valencia, California, surely signals the greatest leap forward in automaton development since Petrouchka; for one thing, it will obviate the need for anyone actually to meet Warhol."

—A. M. O'SULLIVAN

"Andy is terribly tight with his money."　　　　—DOTSON RADER

(See also: Henry Kissinger)

JACK WARNER
"Jack Warner would rather make a bad joke than a good picture."

—JACK BENNY

"Ever had dinner with Louis B. Mayer or Jack Warner? They should have troughs."　　　　—JOAN CRAWFORD

"Now the report is that Harry is planning to fire Jack and just call it Warner Brother."　　　　—NUNNALLY JOHNSON

"He bore no grudge against those he had wronged."

—SIMONE SIGNORET

GEORGE WASHINGTON
"If ever a nation was debauched by a man, the American nation has been debauched by Washington. If ever a nation has suffered from the improper influence of a man, the American nation has suffered from the influence of Washington. If ever a nation was deceived by a man, the American nation has been deceived by Washington. Let his conduct then be an example to future ages. Let the history of the Federal Government instruct mankind that the masque of patriotism may be worn to conceal the foulest designs against the liberties of the people."

—B. F. BACHE

"Every hero becomes a bore at last."

—RALPH WALDO EMERSON

"Did anyone ever see Washington nude? It is inconceivable."

—NATHANIEL HAWTHORNE

"Washington is the last person you'd ever suspect of having been a young man."　　　　—SAMUEL ELIOT MORISON

"How is it that George Washington slept so many places and yet never told a lie?"
—LAURENCE J. PETER

(See also: Alexander Hamilton, Patrick Henry)

WASHINGTON REDSKINS

(See entry: George McGovern)

BOB WATERFIELD
"Cold to everyone except my mother, and she was only around during Thanksgiving and Christmas."
—JANE RUSSELL

JAMES WATT
"He is an incredibly slimy character."
—ANSEL ADAMS

"A man whose neck I'd love to wring"
—ALFRED KNOPF

"His plan to open a billion acres of offshore lands for oil exploration will result in the beginning of surfing in Colorado."
—MARK RUSSELL

"He's off making a science-fiction sequel to *E.T.* It's called *Raiders of the Last Park.*"
—PETE WILSON

(See also: Paul Shaffer)

EVELYN WAUGH
"His style has the desperate jauntiness of an orchestra fiddling away for dear life on a sinking ship."
—EDMUND WILSON

JOHN WAYNE
"In a manner of speaking, John Wayne was me if I had been a mediocre, overpaid actor."
—JIM BISHOP

"He walks like a fairy. He's the only man in the world who can do that."
—WILLIAM WELLMAN

CLIFTON WEBB
"It must be tough to be orphaned at seventy-one!"
—NOEL COWARD

CASPAR WEINBERGER
"What you have is a guy who by the very bluster with which he talks convinces you he can't be real."
—NEWT GINGRICH

"He's lost all credibility. Instead of Cap the Knife, he's Cap the Ladle."
—ALBERT GORE, JR.

113

RAQUEL WELCH
"One of her major talents is the ability to stand up on stage without pitching over." —MARVIN KITMAN

"The only reaction she is capable of registering on-camera is one of fright; she depicts this emotion by suddenly opening her mouth as wide as she can." —HARRY and MICHAEL MEDVED,
co-founders of the Golden Turkey Awards

ORSON WELLES
"If there were a real mind in charge of the production as a whole, Orson Welles would be the greatest assistant director of all time."
—ERIC BENTLEY

"Everything about him was oversized, including his ego."
—JOAN FONTAINE

"You—effeminate guys of the theater, what do you know about real war!" —ERNEST HEMINGWAY

"As an emotional actor, Welles is without insight, accuracy, power, or grace. In short, without talent . . ." —WALTER KERR

"There, but for the grace of God, goes God."
—HERMAN J. MANKIEWICZ

"There is nothing about the work of Orson Welles to convince us that he has ever felt humility or love anywhere except in front of a mirror."
—JOHN SIMON

H. G. WELLS
"An egotistical Englishman who held his nose at everything American—except money" —HEDDA HOPPER

MAE WEST
"Seductive and reeling motions reminiscent of an overfed python"
—GRAHAM GREENE

NATHANAEL WEST
"I wonder if he's long winded as a defense mechanism."
—F. SCOTT FITZGERALD

JAMES McNEILL WHISTLER
"Too much mind, or what he thought was mind"
—SHERWOOD ANDERSON

"People will forgive anything but beauty and talent. So I am doubly unpardonable."　　　　　　　　　—JAMES McNEILL WHISTLER

"As for borrowing Mr. Whistler's ideas about art, the only thoroughly original ideas I have ever heard him express have had reference to his own superiority as a painter over painters greater than himself."
　　　　　　　　　—OSCAR WILDE

WHISTLER'S MOTHER
"Volatile, bombastic and domineering"　　　　—ROGER CORMAN

STUART WHITMAN
"Perpetually numb"　　　　　　　　　—JUDITH CRIST

WALT WHITMAN
"The author should be kicked from all decent society as below the level of the brute. He must be some escaped lunatic raving in pitiable delirium."　　　　　　　—*The Boston Intelligencer,* 1855

"Whitman's argument seems to be that because a prairie is wide debauchery is admirable, and because the Mississippi is long every American is God."　　　　　　　—SIDNEY LANIER

THE WHO
"Loudest pop group"　　　—*The Guinness Book of World Records*

OSCAR WILDE
"Do you realize that an anagram for 'Oscar Wilde,' which could also be the first line of a suppressed poem by him, is 'O lad I screw'?"
　　　　　　　　　—DICK CAVETT

"Odd that such brilliant wit should be allied to no humor at all"
　　　　　　　　　—NOEL COWARD

"Oscar, bourgeois malgré lui."　　　—JAMES MCNEILL WHISTLER
　　　　　　　　　(See also: Gore Vidal)

WILHELM II OF GERMANY
"To see the Kaiser's epitaph
Would make a weeping willow laugh."　　　—OLIVER HERFORD

"I do remember being delighted when Kitchener was drowned. I wasn't a critic of his, you understand, but I confused him with the Kaiser; they looked alike."　　　　　—ROBERT MORLEY

CINDY WILLIAMS
"She has been like a foreign being to me."　　—PENNY MARSHALL

ESTHER WILLIAMS
"Wet she's a star."   —FANNY BRICE

PAUL WILLIAMS
"Paul's very superstitious. He considers it unlucky to walk under a black cat."   —PAT McCORMICK

"One time Katy locked me out. I got back in through the puppy door."
—PAUL WILLIAMS

TENNESSEE WILLIAMS
"Playwright Tennessee Williams often writes like an arrested adolescent who disarmingly imagines that he will attain stature if (as short boys are advised in Dixie) he loads enough manure in his shoes."
—*TIME*

DON WILSON
"An elephantine announcer"   —MAURICE ZOLOTOW

EARL WILSON
"He has a strange growth on his neck—his head."
—ARTHUR GODFREY

HAROLD WILSON
"If Harold Wilson ever went to school without any boots, it was merely because he was too big for them."
—HAROLD MacMILLAN

WOODROW WILSON
"How can I talk to a fellow who thinks himself the first man in two thousand years to know anything about peace on earth?"
—GEORGES CLEMENCEAU

"The University president who cashiered every professor unwilling to support Woodrow Wilson for the first vacancy in the Trinity"
—H. L. MENCKEN

"A Byzantine logothete"   —THEODORE ROOSEVELT

"I feel certain that he would not recognize a generous impulse if he met it on the street."   —WILLIAM HOWARD TAFT

WALTER WINCHELL
"I don't see why Walter Winchell is allowed to live."
—ETHEL BARRYMORE

"Has anyone ever criticized you for bleating over the radio week- and two-week-old news, and yelping 'Scoop!' or 'Exclusive!'?"
—W. C. FIELDS

"Winchell appeals to the whims of the younger degeneration."
—WILLIAM RANDOLPH HEARST

"A New Enemy of the New Germany"   —ADOLF HITLER

"I can't wait to speak at Winchell's funeral."   —GEORGE JESSEL
(Winchell wasn't dead yet)

"Gent's room journalist"   —WESTBROOK PEGLER

"A cringing coward"   —ED SULLIVAN

THE DUCHESS OF WINDSOR
"You can't make the Duchess of Windsor into Rebecca of Sunnybrook Farm. The facts of life are very stubborn things."
—CLEVELAND AMORY

THE DUKE OF WINDSOR
(*See entry:* H. R. H. Edward, Duke of Windsor)

DAVE WINFIELD
"The biggest feet in baseball"   —LOU PINIELLA

SHELLEY WINTERS
"Well, if I'm your favorite author, then you really must be from Hollywood because that means you're practically illiterate."
—DOROTHY PARKER

THOMAS WOLFE
"Thomas Wolfe was half-baked and Hemingway remained a raw egg."
—LEON EDEL

BOB WOODWARD
(*See entry:* Carl Bernstein and Bob Woodward)

ALEXANDER WOOLLCOTT
"This New Jersey Nero who mistakes his pinafore for a toga"
—EDNA FERBER

"A persnickety fellow with more fizz than brains"   —BEN HECHT

"There was nobody in public life easier to caricature until Adolf Hitler came along, with the possible exception of George Bernard Shaw."
—HARPO MARX

"Alexander Woollcott says good writers should never use the word 'very.' Nuts to Alexander Woollcott." —H. ALLEN SMITH

"Old Vitriol and Violets" —JAMES THURBER

(See also: Robert Benchley)

FAY WRAY

"During a dramatic episode in which a certain Miss Wray lay gibbering across Mr. Kong's wrist, my companion, in a voice shrill with irritation, cried out, 'I can't think what he sees in her.'"

—QUENTIN CRISP

(See also: San Diego Padres)

JANE WYATT

"One of the dumber stars" —GRAHAM GREENE

JANE WYMAN

(See entry: Ronald Reagan)

X

DENG XIAOPING

"Cold and even ruthless appreciation of the uses of power"
—ZBIGNIEW BRZEZINSKI

Y

HENNY YOUNGMAN

"The greatest form of flattering is imitation, and one of Henny's unusual traits is that he is flattered by the fact that for many years he has been an imitation of a comedian." —MILTON BERLE

Z

PIA ZADORA

"The chairman's breakfast" —JAMES BRADY

PIA ZADORA and MESHULAM RIKLIS

"And we know Pia and Riklis were *born* to be the butt of a thousand jokes." —SUZY

DARRYL F. ZANUCK

"If there is such a thing as the Napoleonic complex, Zanuck possesses it in full measure." —GARSON KANIN

"He liked women and was happily married but women's problems and feelings bored him totally." —OTTO PREMINGER

"Whenever the publicity department calls me a genius, I always remind them of the time I refused to sign Gable because I thought his ears were too big. Some genius." —DARRYL F. ZANUCK

RON ZIEGLER

"I found Ziegler to be stubborn, unpleasant, barely competent, and power hungry . . ." —JEB STUART MAGRUDER

EMILE ZOLA

"Mr. Zola is determined to show that, if he has not genius, he can at least be dull." —OSCAR WILDE

"Perfection is such a nuisance that I often regret having cured myself of using tobacco." —EMILE ZOLA

ADOLPH ZUKOR

"Would I comment on Mr. Zukor's 'visual style'? Well, he knew the color of money. No, I didn't say that . . ." —PETER BOGDANOVICH